York Notes Rapid Revision

Love and Relationships Poetry Anthology

AQA GCSE English Literature

Written by Lucy Toop

YORK PRESS
322 Old Brompton Road, London SW5 9JH

PEARSON EDUCATION LIMITED
80 Strand, London, WC2R 0RL

10 9 8 7 6 5 4 3 2 1

ISBN 978–1–2922–7093–7

Phototypeset by DTP Media
Printed in Slovakia

Text credits:
'Letters from Yorkshire' by Maura Dooley, from *Sound Barrier: Poems 1982-2002* (Bloodaxe Books, 2002). Reproduced with kind permission of Bloodaxe Books. 'Eden Rock' by Charles Causley, from *Collected Poems 1951-2000*, Picador, 2000. 'Walking Away' from Selected Poems by C Day Lewis, reprinted by permission of Peters Fraser & Dunlop (www.petersfraserdunlop.com) on behalf of the estate of C Day Lewis. 'Follower' from Opened Ground: Selected poems 1966-1996 by Seamus Heaney. Copyright © 1998 Seamus Heaney. Reprinted by permission of Farrar, Straus and Giroux and of Faber and Faber Ltd. 'Before You Were Mine' from *Mean Time* by Carol Ann Duffy. Published by Anvil Press Poetry, 1993. Copyright © Carol Ann Duffy. Reproduced by permission of the author c/o Rogers, Coleridge & White Ltd., 20 Powis Mews, London, W11 1JN. 'Winter Swans' from *Skirrid Hill* by Owen Sheers. Published by Seren, 2005. Copyright © Owen Sheers. Reproduced by permission of the author c/o Rogers, Coleridge & White Ltd., 20 Powis Mews, London, W11 1JN. 'Mother, Any Distance' from *Book of Matches* by Simon Armitage and 'Singh Song!' from *Look, We Have Coming to Dover!* by Daljit Nagra reproduced by kind permission of Faber and Faber Ltd. 'Climbing My Grandfather' by Andrew Waterhouse from *In*, Andrew Waterhouse, The Rialto, 2000, reproduced by kind permission of The Rialto.

Photo credits:
Constantinis / © iStock for page 5 bottom / Predrag Popovski/Shutterstock for page 6 middle / Subbotina Anna/Shutterstock for page 9 bottom / MIGUEL GARCIA SAAVEDRA/Shutterstock for page 14 middle / neenawat khenyothaa/Shutterstock for page 17 bottom / Katerina Fabianova/Shutterstock for page 21 bottom / Rawpixel.com/Shutterstock for page 25 top / Harsanyi Andras/Shutterstock for page 30 bottom / thomasmales/ © iStock for page 33 bottom / BIGANDT.COM/Shutterstock for page 34 middle / SteAck/Shutterstock for page 37 bottom / Dado Photos/Shutterstock for page 38 middle / Aleksandr Sulga/Shutterstock for page 41 bottom / colin13362/Shutterstock for page 42 middle / DenisProduction.com/Shutterstock for page 45 middle / Everett Historical/Shutterstock for page 49 bottom / DarkBird/Shutterstock for page 50 middle / dwphotos/Shutterstock for page 53 bottom / Philip Lee Harvey/©IStock for page 54 middle / alina_danilova/Shutterstock for page 58 middle / Rauluminate/© iStock for page 61 bottom / PhonlamaiPhoto/© iStock for page 66 middle / Vixit/Shutterstock for page 68 middle / greenair/Shutterstock for page 70 middle / Simon Kadula/Shutterstock for page 72 top / J. Lekavicius/Shutterstock for page 74 middle

CONTENTS

WHEN WE TWO PARTED by Lord Byron

Lord Byron was once described as 'mad, bad, and dangerous to know', though he doesn't sound it in this **lyric**, which probably refers to a real past mistress. More importantly, it reflects the emotional intensity and melancholy **imagery** of love and death common to the **Romantic movement**.

Metre (here **dactylic**) is used to create a heavy and doom-laden **mood**, like a funeral procession

Use of pronoun 'we' to emphasise they are now 'parted' – 'two', not 'one'

'Half' is ambiguous. Were they both half-relieved (to end it)? Or was only one of them (him) 'broken-hearted'?

When we two parted
In silence and tears,
Half broken-hearted
To sever for years,
5   Pale grew thy cheek and cold,
Colder thy kiss;
Truly that hour foretold
Sorrow to this.

The dew of the morning
10   Sank chill on my brow –
It felt like the warning
Of what I feel now.
Thy vows are all broken,
And light is thy fame;
15   I hear thy name spoken,
And share in its shame.

'Sever' suggests violent and complete separation

Imagery of death (here and throughout) echoes feelings of loss and sorrow

Past and present: he feels the pain as sharply now as he did then

The weak (or 'feminine') **rhyme** of 'morning' and 'warning' could emphasise his mixed feelings towards her

Betrayal and false love: as reflected in the idea of 'broken vows'

Alliterative sibilance of 'sh' echoes the whispering gossip that he hears

4

Use of pronouns – 'they', 'thee', 'me' – suggests feelings of separation and isolation

Use of 'knell' (bell rung at death) emphasises the 'death' of the relationship

'Shudder' implies disgust or horror at thought of her

> They name thee before me,
> A knell in mine ear;
> A shudder come o'er me –
> 20 Why wert thou so dear?
> They know not I knew thee,
> Who knew thee too well –
> Long, long shall I rue thee,
> Too deeply to tell.
>
> 25 In secret we met –
> In silence I grieve,
> That thy heart could forget,
> Thy spirit deceive.
> If I should meet thee
> 30 After long years,
> How should I greet thee?
> With silence and tears.

Rhetorical question implies that the speaker can't believe his earlier feelings of love

Changing tenses 'know'/'knew', like 'felt'/'feel' in ll.11–12, echoes changing emotions

Long vowel sound of 'rue' echoes length of regret

Strong feelings (of hate or love): these may be felt 'too deeply' to describe to others

Silent 'grief' suggests she is dead to him, and he has suffered by repressing his feelings

Question suggests feelings of discomfort and unease

Repetition of earlier phrase shows renewal of pain – and perhaps an inability to move on

Disrupted **rhythm** in final **stanza**, almost as if speaker is suppressing sobs

What is the poem's setting?

- The poem recalls a **past love affair** from **'years'** ago. Byron doesn't specify time or place – some readers believe he was protecting the identity of a real-life past lover.
- Hearing others talk about his ex-lover has revived **bitter memories** for the speaker.

What is the poem about?

- The speaker describes his **mixed feelings** on hearing rumours about a past love.
- The speaker compares his **sorrow** at how his lover's feelings for him **'grew ... cold'** when they **separated**, to the way he feels now when **'they name thee before me'**.
- Nobody else knew about their affair – suggesting it was **secret**, perhaps even **illicit** – and so he now has to listen to comments about her all around him.
- It's partly this that makes him **'shudder'** now, but also the fact **she has moved on**.
- He feels **betrayed** by her current behaviour, just as he did years ago; he's ashamed he loved someone so **deceitful**.

Five key things about the language

1. Byron's use of pronouns shifts between **'we'**, **'thee'** and **'I'**, reflecting present separation, but also the way their secret past separates them from everyone else.
2. The mostly regular **dactylic** metre could reflect ideas about the inevitable death of love, only slipping in the final **stanza** where some beats are dropped in lines 1, 5 and 6.
3. The speaker describes his ex-lover using typically Romantic vocabulary associated with death – **'pale'**, **'cold'**, **'knell'** – to represent their love.
4. Most of Byron's rhymes are strong, emphasising endings, but weak rhymes in the second stanza – **'morning'/'warning'**, **'broken'/'spoken'** – could suggest the speaker's feelings are not as clear as he states.
5. Repetition of words and rhymes e.g. **'tears'/'years'**, hints at the inescapability of the speaker's feelings: he is doomed to grieve past love, even though he tries to escape his memories.

Five key quotations

1. Pain of separation: 'To sever for years', l.4: 'severs' suggests that passion may end violently and suddenly.
2. Betrayal: 'Thy vows are all broken', l.13: implies that the lover was not true to her word.
3. Painful memories: 'A knell in mine ear', l.18: hearing a past love's name renews the agony of loss.
4. Power of emotion: 'Long, long shall I rue thee, Too deeply to tell', l.23: the sorrow of separation is both lasting and impossible to describe.
5. Uncertainty: 'How should I greet thee?', l.31: implies anxiety about how he will behave if they should meet again.

Note it!

Compare how Byron presents ideas about the end of relationships with Hardy's ideas in 'Neutral Tones'. Are their feelings equally 'dead'?

Exam focus

How can I write about how Byron uses imagery? AO2

You can explore how Byron uses imagery to present past love.

> Byron's use of death imagery reflects the speaker's belief that the relationship is dead. His lover's 'cold' kiss mirrors his 'chill' brow, implying that their feelings have died, her name nothing but a 'knell' when he hears it. However, his ongoing 'tears' could suggest that he finds it hard to let go of his feelings, even though the relationship has been over for some years now.

Topic sentence makes clear point about the theme of endings

Precise references all support the point being made

Signals an alternative interpretation of developed idea

Link to wider context

Now you try!

Finish this paragraph about betrayal. Use one of the quotations from the list.

Byron implies that the speaker's lover has betrayed him. He does this by . . . .

LOVE'S PHILOSOPHY by Percy Bysshe Shelley

The poem follows a tradition of European poetry making a playful argument in favour of giving in to love – and uses the nature **imagery** that was so popular in the **Romantic movement**.

Words like 'mingle' suggest gentleness at the beginning

Weak rhyme could suggest that two similar but not identical things, e.g. male and female, can mix

Nature imagery pervades the poem, while **enjambment** emphasises the sense of a natural 'flow' between different things

Confident statement advances persuasive **tone**

Love is natural: set by 'divine law'; this links to Romantic ideas about the authority of love

'Being' implies that the 'mingling' is not purely physical, but something more spiritual

Rhetorical question undermines objections to kissing!

Passionate verbs – 'clasp' and 'kiss' – make the argument more explicitly physical

Desire: using nature to comment on human desire, he implies his desire is pure whereas her reluctance is 'unnatural'

Strong rhyme ends the poem – and the argument – with certainty

Implies the addressee is acting cruelly

Repetition of 'kiss' and 'clasp' and other 'joining' verbs makes the idea seem more acceptable

> The fountains mingle with the river
> And the rivers with the ocean,
> The winds of heaven mix for ever
> With a sweet emotion;
> 5   Nothing in the world is single,
> All things by a law divine
> In one another's being mingle –
> Why not I with thine?
>
> See the mountains kiss high heaven,
> 10   And the waves clasp one another;
> No sister-flower would be forgiven
> If it disdain'd its brother;
> And the sunlight clasps the earth,
> And the moonbeams kiss the sea –
> 15   What are all these kissings worth
> If thou kiss not me?

What is the poem's setting?

- The speaker uses **nature** to argue that it is natural for humans to kiss and **'mingle'**.

- The poem **may** have a **real addressee**, but also follows an established poetic convention of male speakers persuading women to sleep with them (like Marvell's 'To His Coy Mistress').

What is the poem about?

- The poem opens with images of **'fountains'**, **'rivers'** and **'the ocean'**, reminding us of the **natural flow** and **purity** of water.

- The speaker argues that **mixing** is a **natural state**, set by an unspecified **'law divine'**. By talking about 'beings' mingling rather than 'bodies', he draws the **argument** away from the purely physical, suggesting a meeting of minds.

- The second stanza introduces more physically **passionate** words such as **'clasp'** and **'kiss'**, reminding us this is what the speaker really wants.

- The **tone** becomes more **demanding** as the speaker compares the addressee unfavourably to a **'sister-flower'**, that grows alongside its **'brother'**.

- The final question introduces a more **plaintive note**, as the speaker feels that **everything** in the world is being kissed except him!

Five key things about the language

1. As we'd expect from a Romantic poet, Shelley uses a great deal of nature imagery, from the vast **'ocean'** to the tiny **'sister-flower'**, from **'sunlight'** to **'moonbeams'**.

2. A mixture of strong and weak rhyme – or 'masculine' and 'feminine' rhyme, as they're sometimes called – echoes the thinly veiled theme of sex.

3. A **semantic field** of mixing is repeated throughout the poem to emphasise the point: **'mingle'**, **'mix'**, **'kiss'**, **'clasp'**.

4. Both stanzas end with questions, which can be read as assertive and demanding, or as genuine puzzlement.

5. The speaker moves from the **universal**, e.g. **'all things'**, to the **personal** at the end of each stanza, e.g. to **'I'** and **'thine'**, reminding us of his goal.

Five key quotations

1. Emphasis on feeling: **'With a sweet emotion'**, l.4: the argument may be logical, but the feelings are what's important.

2. Naturalness of sex and love: **'Nothing in the world is single'**, l.5: men and women are meant to love.

3. Rightness of love: **'... by a law divine'**, l.6: humans are designed to be together by a higher power.

4. Kindness: **'No sister-flower would be forgiven / If it disdain'd its brother'**, ll.11–12: the object of love should take pity on the lover.

5. Unrequited love: **'What are all these kissings worth'**, l.15: unrequited love makes the world seem bleak and without value.

Note it!

Compare how Shelley presents physical desire with the way that Barrett Browning does in 'Sonnet 29'. How do their requests for their lover's presence differ?

Exam focus

How can I write about Shelley's use of rhyme in the poem?

You can show how Shelley's use of rhyme is linked to Romantic ideas.

> By saying that 'Nothing in the world is single', Shelley echoes a Romantic idea that men and women should love freely. He uses 'masculine' and 'feminine' rhyme to support this argument, balancing 'single' and 'mingle' against 'divine' and 'thine' to show the rhymes almost literally 'clasping'. By building ideas of 'male' and 'female' into the form of the poem, he emphasises how we should see love as a natural part of life.

- Clear point linking idea to context
- Examples support the point being made
- Links form back to contextual ideas

Now you try!

Finish this paragraph about unrequited love. Use one of the quotations from the list.

Shelley suggests that, without love, life is meaningless. ....

My progress   Needs more work ☐   Getting there ☐   Sorted! ☐

SPECIAL FOCUS 1: Sound and rhythm

What are sound and rhythm?

- Poets often choose **specific words** because of the **effect** of particular **letter sounds**, e.g. words beginning with **plosive** *p* or *b* can sound **harsh and aggressive**.
- The **rhythm** of a poem is created by the **positioning** of words to create **stresses** or **beats**.

How do I identify them in a poem like 'Love's Philosophy'?

- Read the poem **aloud**, looking for words which are given **emphasis** by the poem's rhythm, e.g. **'mix'** (l.3), **'why'**, **'I'** and **'thine'** (l.8).
- Think about how the poet **disrupts the rhythm** of the poem, e.g. at the start of l.12 to accentuate the harsh word **'disdain'd'**.
- Look at the poet's use of **punctuation**, e.g. **enjambment** between ll.6 and 7 lengthens the long vowel in **'divine'**.
- Think about ways in which the **sound** of words adds to their impact, e.g. the **alliteration** of **'m'** in the first **stanza** could be interpreted as echoing moans of longing.

Exam focus

How can I write about sound and rhythm?

You could use verbs and adjectives related to sound and rhythm: *regular, irregular, constant, disrupt, harsh, soft, rapid, slow, emphatic, dramatic.*

> For most of the poem, Shelley uses irregular beats to suggest hesitant thoughtfulness, e.g. between lines 3 and 4. However, in the final four lines, the rhythm falls into a regular iambic metre: it's as if the speaker is becoming more emphatic in his demands, and the steady beat suggests a pulsing desire to 'kiss' and 'clasp'.

Focus on rhythm

How rhythm changes

Exploration of effect

Now you try!

Think about the other poems in the cluster. Do any use sound or rhythm to emphasise key ideas?

PORPHYRIA'S LOVER by Robert Browning

Browning's **dramatic monologue** presents a speaker who is revealed as increasingly unstable, both emotionally and morally, as he reaches a point where murder becomes an expression of love. Some readers have even seen the figure of 'Porphyria' as a **personification** of the speaker's mental illness.

Personification of wind sets an eerie **tone**, and **pathetic fallacy** hints at the speaker's unstable emotions

Use of **end-stopping** and enjambment to mirror the speaker's mixed emotions beneath the regular rhyme and **metre**

Active verbs attached to Porphyria, not the speaker, contrasting her power to change the **mood** with his passivity and watchfulness

Regular **rhyme scheme** (ababb, etc.) and (mostly) **iambic tetrameter** could imply speaker's rigid thought patterns

Adjective 'soiled' implies dirt, and perhaps also sin

The speaker talks of himself here and in l.28 in the third person to distance himself

Sexual **imagery** linked to Porphyria suggests her 'soiled' state and the speaker's arousal; he later uses her hair, symbolising female sexuality, to strangle her

Gentle, soft verb – the speaker may want a clearer demonstration of love

Jealousy: the speaker presents Porphyria as kept from him by the world

The rain set early in to-night,
     The sullen wind was soon awake,
It tore the elm-tops down for spite,
     And did its worst to vex the lake:
5   I listened with heart fit to break.
When glided in Porphyria; straight
     She shut the cold out and the storm,
And kneeled and made the cheerless grate
     Blaze up, and all the cottage warm;
10   Which done, she rose, and from her form
Withdrew the dripping cloak and shawl,
     And laid her soiled gloves by, untied
Her hat and let the damp hair fall,
     And, last, she sat down by my side
15   And called me. When no voice replied,
She put my arm about her waist,
     And made her smooth white shoulder bare,
And all her yellow hair displaced,
     And, stooping, made my cheek lie there,
20   And spread, o'er all, her yellow hair,
Murmuring how she loved me – she
     Too weak, for all her heart's endeavour,
To set its struggling passion free
     From pride, and vainer ties dissever,
25   And give herself to me for ever.

12

But passion sometimes would prevail,
    Nor could to-night's gay feast restrain
A sudden thought of one so pale
    For love of her, and all in vain:
30   So, she was come through wind and rain.
Be sure I looked up at her eyes
    Happy and proud; at last I knew
Porphyria worshipped me; surprise
    Made my heart swell, and still it grew
35   While I debated what to do.
That moment she was mine, mine, fair,
    Perfectly pure and good: I found
A thing to do, and all her hair
    In one long yellow string I wound
40   Three times her little throat around,
And strangled her. No pain felt she;
    I am quite sure she felt no pain.
As a shut bud that holds a bee,
    I warily oped her lids: again
45   Laughed the blue eyes without a stain.
And I untightened next the tress
    About her neck; her cheek once more
Blushed bright beneath my burning kiss:
    I propped her head up as before,
50   Only, this time my shoulder bore
Her head, which droops upon it still:
    The smiling rosy little head,
So glad it has its utmost will,
    That all it scorned at once is fled,
55   And I, its love, am gained instead!
Porphyria's love: she guessed not how
    Her darling one wish would be heard.
And thus we sit together now,
    And all night long we have not stirred,
60   And yet God has not said a word!

Annotations:

- Eyes used to symbolise life and truth to the speaker, here and in l.45
- **Narrative** shift from Porphyria being active to the speaker being active signals a turning point
- Obsession: repetition of 'mine' reveals the speaker's possessiveness
- Euphemistic wording distances the murder
- Contrast of **enjambment** to describe murder and short clause to justify; the pause could suggest uncertainty
- Insecurity: the short sentence implies the need to convince himself
- **Simile** suggests *his* fear and her power
- Language suggests heated passion, as if in death, she comes alive for him
- Echo of earlier action shows roles are reversed
- First use of pronoun 'we' shows they are now truly 'together'
- Ambiguity of final sentence leaves us uncertain of the speaker's mood

PORPHYRIA'S LOVER by Robert Browning

What is the poem's setting?

- The speaker sits alone in a cold cottage, **symbolising isolation** – the wind reflects his feelings of **resentment** and vexation.
- The **'spite'** of the wind could imply he views his absent lover as **selfish**, and also **foreshadows** his later **violence** in murdering her.

What is the poem about?

- The speaker's heart is **'fit to break'** – we can guess later that he's been **imagining** Porphyria with **other men**.
- When Porphyria arrives, she makes the room **'warm'**, implying her **warm nature** and **desire**, but her actions leave the speaker **unmoved** and silent, so she tries harder to please him.

- The speaker finally sees 'worship' of him in her eyes and, aroused, decides how he can **keep** her for himself alone. He **strangles** her with her own hair.
- Describing the murder **calmly**, the speaker still seems **unsure** of his actions, until he checks her eyes which 'laugh' without **'a stain'**, **absolving** him of the crime.
- The speaker now feels able to **act** upon his desire and hold Porphyria, telling himself she now has her **'darling one wish'**; and the poem ends with them sitting together, waiting.

Five key things about the language

1. This is a **narrative** poem, with a structure moving from separation to togetherness; Browning uses the **dramatic monologue** form to reveal the speaker's emotions.
2. Regular rhyme creates a sense that the speaker is unable to free himself from feelings of jealousy. The five-line structure is uneasy and feels irregular – like the speaker's moral beliefs.
3. **Enjambment** allows the words to flow naturally over the rhyme, but Browning also uses it to highlight emotion.
4. Pathetic fallacy emphasises the speaker's isolation from society and 'normal' human behaviour.
5. The use of physical and sexual **imagery** throughout reveals the speaker's sexual obsession, as well as his desire to keep Porphyria 'pure'.

14

Five key quotations

1. Pain of love: 'I listened with heart fit to break', l.5: longing brings an almost physical pain.
2. Sexual love: 'And all her yellow hair displaced', l.18: image of female sexuality unbound, literally and **figuratively**.
3. Barriers to love: '... set its struggling passion free from pride', ll.23–4: love may be held back by social convention.
4. Power/Possessive love: 'And give herself to me for ever', l.25: the speaker wants to keep her for himself alone.
5. Obsessive love: '... at last I knew / Porphyria worshipped me', ll.32–3: the speaker wants to be the sole focus of love; to feel godlike.

Note it!

Compare how Browning presents frustrated love with how Charlotte Mew does in 'The Farmer's Bride'. Do we feel the same sympathy for both speakers?

Exam focus

How can I write about desire in this poem?

You can use Browning's description of Porphyria.

> The speaker's language makes it clear his lover's actions are erotically charged for him: she bares 'her smooth white shoulder' to him and loosens her 'yellow hair'. References to her body reveal his focus, while the verbs suggest she is actively seducing him. However, there is also a sense that he fears and despises her for this, describing her gloves as 'soiled', implying she is 'dirty' or 'used'.

Topic sentence makes clear point linked to language

Carefully chosen quotations as evidence

Exploration of effect

Alternative reading adds depth

Now you try!

Finish this paragraph about power. Use one of the quotations from the list.

Browning's language reveals that the speaker wishes to have power over Porphyria. He says that ....

My progress Needs more work ☐ Getting there ☐ Sorted! ☐

SONNET 29 – 'I THINK OF THEE!'
by Elizabeth Barrett Browning

Already a successful and popular poet herself, here Barrett Browning addresses her husband, the poet Robert Browning. It is one of forty-four **sonnets**, which he encouraged her to publish as *Sonnets from the Portuguese*, despite her initial fear that they were too personal.

Short, exclamatory sentence which begins the poem is arresting – is she in pain, or joyful?

Imagery of growth and flowering suggests she 'flourishes' with him

Extended metaphor (husband = tree, her thoughts = vines twined around it) suggests her thoughts are overwhelming

Comparison to biblical tree suggests he is king-like in her eyes, as well as tall, strong and fruitful

Regeneration: his return will revive and sustain their love

Look at the verbs: 'should' is almost reproachful, while 'rustle' could be imploring or demanding

'Bands' and 'insphere' imply that her thoughts choke and constrain reality

Words of life – 'breathe' and 'air' – also echo the biblical idea of 'a new heaven'

> I think of thee! – my thoughts do twine and bud
> About thee, as wild vines, about a tree,
> Put out broad leaves, and soon there's nought to see
> Except the straggling green which hides the wood.
> 5   Yet, O my palm-tree, be it understood
> I will not have my thoughts instead of thee
> Who art dearer, better! Rather, instantly
> Renew thy presence; as a strong tree should,
> Rustle thy boughs and set thy trunk all bare,
> 10 And let these bands of greenery which insphere thee
> Drop heavily down,– burst, shattered, everywhere!
> Because, in this deep joy to see and hear thee
> And breathe within thy shadow a new air,
> I do not think of thee – I am too near thee.

Barrett Browning breaks out of the traditional **octave-sestet** division of the sonnet form and extends the completing couplet to three lines

Sexually loaded vocabulary is strikingly direct, implying sexual satisfaction

Delight: she proudly expresses preference for real, physical love over dreams

Circular form echoes the beginning of the poem, but the changed wording suggests resolution

16

What is the poem's setting?

- It is very likely that Barrett Browning herself is the speaker in this poem which expresses **longing** for her husband's return from an unspecified **absence**: has he been gone a long time, or only a few hours?
- The **passionate** statement of **nourishing love** reflects the **inspirational** effect they had on each other's writing.

What is the poem about?

- Addressing her **absent husband**, the speaker describes her thoughts as so strong that they threaten to overpower the **memory** of him.
- She makes it clear that she would rather have him present than spend her time **thinking** about him.
- She urges him to return and clear away her thoughts, implying that – as a good husband – he should be with her. She longs to **lose herself** in his presence.
- The language implies she will **'drop'**, **'burst'** and 'shatter' at his return, hinting at **sexual desire**. It suggests her love is **all-consuming**, but also **renewing**. She feels reborn with him.
- She ends where she began, with a reference to her thoughts, but this time expresses her **joy** at leaving them behind to become one with him.

Five key things about the language

1. Nature imagery throughout emphasises their love is natural and fruitful, implying that sexual love is healthy.

2. Bending the poem's sonnet form by shifting the **volta** and extending the couplet shows that the poet understands 'the rules' but is willing to break free to follow her feelings.

3. **Run-on** lines echo the vocabulary of 'bursting' through boundaries.

4. The extended metaphor of the tree and vine runs through the poem like a trunk, with biblical allusions echoing the imagery of 'The Song of Songs' or the Garden of Eden.

5. Reversal of the opening lines at the end of the poem mirrors her feelings of completion with her husband.

Five key quotations

1. **Longing:** '... the straggling green which hides the wood', l.4: her imagination threatens to overwhelm her with loss when he is absent.

2. **Female perspective:** '... as a strong tree should', l.8: suggests she wishes her husband to take control.

3. **Passion:** '... set thy trunk all bare', l.9: she is not afraid to suggest that sexual desire is healthy.

4. **Satisfaction in marriage:** '... this deep joy', l.12: the feeling of true love is one of completion, almost religious in depth.

5. **Self-sacrifice:** '... breathe within thy shadow a new air', l.13: true love does not seek to dominate and stifle.

Note it!

Compare how Barrett Browning here and Hardy in 'Neutral Tones' use nature to present feelings. Does Hardy offer any sense of love as a source of life?

Exam focus

How can I write about a female perspective of love? (AO2) (AO3)

You can use Barrett Browning's use of metaphor to explore this.

> Barrett Browning's image of her husband as a 'strong tree' sees her as a vine growing around him, which implies her acceptance of nineteenth-century attitudes to male dominance. However, the openness of her passionate imagery as she demands that he set his 'trunk all bare', and the fact she eloped with him in the first place, suggests that she is not afraid to break convention by expressing her desires.

Opening links language and social context clearly

Signals an alternative reading

Use of specific context used relevantly

Makes clear alternative interpretation

Now you try!

Finish this paragraph about marriage. Use one of the quotations from the list.

Barrett Browning shows how much she values the idea of marriage. She describes .....

My progress   Needs more work ☐   Getting there ☐   Sorted! ☐

SPECIAL FOCUS 2: Form and structure

What are form and structure?

- The **form** of a poem is the **type** of poem it is, e.g. **sonnet** (a poetic form typically addressing a lover), **free verse**.
- The **structure** of a poem is the **physical organisation and order** the poem takes around the form, using rhyme, **line length**, etc.

How do I identify them in a poem like 'Sonnet 29'?

- Explore **how** and **why** a poet may have used **a particular form**. Does the poet stick to the 'rules', e.g. why doesn't Barrett Browning end with a couplet?
- Look at **line lengths**, especially in **free verse**. Do any lines stand out? Why?
- Think about the **overall 'shape'** of the poem. Look for narrative **development** or repetition, e.g. Barrett Browning's ending echoes her opening.
- Consider the **rhyme scheme**: is it obvious? Does the poet use **enjambment** or do **end-stopped** lines emphasise words (e.g. **'thee'** in 'Sonnet 29')?
- Look at the **metre**. What **pace** has the poet created? Slow or upbeat?

Exam focus

How can I write about form and structure?

It is crucial to explore **how** form and structure are used rather than simply to identify types of form and structure.

Although Barrett Browning uses the sonnet form, she breaks conventions by changing the traditional structure. Instead of a volta shifting the mood after the octave, it comes, halfway through line seven. Instead of a rhyming couplet, she ends with a triplet. This suggests the strength of her emotions, like her use of enjambment: both show her desire to 'shatter' restraint.	Form/structure words
	Evidence from the poem
	How form and structure work together

Now you try!

Think about the other poems in the cluster. Do any play with form or structure? Why?

NEUTRAL TONES by Thomas Hardy

Hardy's poem – like Byron's – looks back to the end of a relationship, which some readers mistakenly link to his unhappy first marriage. The poem describes a sense of bleak and lonely emptiness that seems the very opposite of love.

Imagery picks up idea of 'neutral' and colourless feelings: nature is dead, like their love

Pronoun suggests unity, but we quickly discover there is no more 'we', emphasising feelings of bitterness

Making God seem mean and petty, creating a sense of lovelessness

We stood by a pond that winter day,
And the sun was white, as though chidden of God,
And a few leaves lay on the starving sod;
   – They had fallen from an ash, and were gray.

Impersonal, 'neutral' phrasing, as if she doesn't feel anything for him

5 Your eyes on me were as eyes that rove
   Over tedious riddles of years ago;
   And some words played between us to and fro
      On which lost the more by our love.

Closed **rhyme scheme** – abba cddc – echoes sense of going nowhere

Bitterness: each focuses on the negatives of the relationship

The smile on your mouth was the deadest thing
10 Alive enough to have strength to die;
   And a grin of bitterness swept thereby
      Like an ominous bird a-wing…

Juxtaposition of the 'deadest' smile which is 'alive' is a paradox which shows things are not as they should be

Could suggest brushing away rubbish, as if she wants to be rid of him

Since then, keen lessons that love deceives,
And wrings with wrong, have shaped to me
15 Your face, and the God curst sun, and a tree,
      And a pond edged with grayish leaves.

Simile emphasises sense of unease and bad luck to come, or perhaps a bird symbolising death, such as a raven

Irregular **metre** enhances the sense of unease, as if someone were stumbling

Poem ends where it started, suggesting a lack of hope or progress

Memory: unhappiness twists ('wrings') memories, perhaps making them less 'neutral' or honest

What is the poem's setting?

- The speaker remembers the **end of a relationship**, linking it to a pond in a dead, wintry landscape: nature offers no life or comfort to the scene.
- The rural setting and theme of **doomed love** are features that can be found in many of Hardy's novels.

What is the poem about?

- The poem opens with **'We stood'**, but the couple don't seem to be together among the fallen leaves. There is **nothing 'romantic'** about this landscape.
- The speaker describes how the woman's eyes passed over him as if she is already **bored** of him. **'Riddles'** and **'played'** suggest games, but they seem to be arguing.
- Neither shows any passion: even her smile seems **dead** in his memory.
- **'Since then'**, the speaker says, **experience** has shown him that love is false, distorting his **memories** of her face with **bitterness**.
- He still looks back at the **bleak** pond with a sense of being lost to God and to love. There is no more **'we'**.

Five key things about the language

1. Imagery of death pervades the poem: the **'white'** sun, the **'starving sod'**, the **'grey'** leaves from the **'ash'** tree.

2. The metre – **anapaestic** in places – is irregular and jolting, as if the speaker's emotions are not as flat as he states.

3. The rhyme scheme in each **stanza** is circular, suggesting imprisonment: the only half-rhyme is **'rove'/'love'**, perhaps suggesting their love was wrong.

4. **Pathetic fallacy** creates a sinister **mood** that hangs over the poem, suggesting love has been blighted, like the earth: the sun is cursed, a bird is **'ominous'**.

5. The poem has a circular structure, beginning and ending with the pond, but imperfectly so, as if the speaker is trapped in a memory, or in bitter emotions.

Five key quotations

1. **Lack of feeling:** 'Your eyes on me were as eyes that rove / Over tedious riddles ...', ll.5–6: she looks at him with restless indifference, not love.

2. **Recrimination:** '... which lost the more by our love', l.8: they're almost competing to see who suffered most.

3. **Death and decay:** 'The smile on your mouth was the deadest thing', l.9: something once lovely has become horrid.

4. **Bitter emotions:** '... keen lessons that love deceives ... have shaped to me your face', ll.13–15: memories have been twisted by sadness.

5. **Lack of joy:** '... the God curst sun', l.15: even the sun has lost its brightness in their eyes.

Note it!

Compare how Hardy presents feelings of separation to the way that Sheers does in 'Winter Swans'. Does Hardy suggest any chance of a reconciliation?

Exam focus

How can I write about Hardy's use of structure in the poem?

You can show how Hardy uses structural repetition to explore the end of the relationship.

> The speaker describes a memory of a relationship ending, beginning and concluding with the same scene by a pond, suggesting he is unable to move on from the past. More than this, by shifting the descriptions slightly – the sun that has been 'chidden' by God to 'the God curst sun' – Hardy may imply that memories are twisted by emotion to become even more bitter, with the word 'curst' hinting at a complete loss of hope.

- Topic sentence makes clear point linking structure and meaning
- Develops point
- Precise quotations illustrate previous point
- Exploration of effect

Now you try!

Finish this paragraph about language effects, using one of the quotations from the list.

Hardy uses negative vocabulary associated with death. He describes ....

My progress   Needs more work ☐   Getting there ☐   Sorted! ☐

SPECIAL FOCUS 3: Mood and tone

What is mood and tone?

- The **mood** or **tone** of a poem is the **atmosphere** or **feeling evoked**.

How do I identify them in a poem like 'Neutral Tones'?

- Explore the **connotations** of **particular words** or **phrases**: **'an ominous bird a-wing'** suggests bad luck – even death.
- Think about how **particular vocabulary is linked**: all the words related to death – **'starving'**, **'ash'**, **'greyish'**, **'deadest'**, etc.
- Consider **voice** and **viewpoint** in the poem – the use of **'your'** emphasises separation from the other.
- Think about the **sound, pace** and **rhythm**: is the poem fast-paced or slow? How does Hardy vary the rhythm throughout?
- Look for **change** or **development** in the mood or tone: how might we read the **lack** of change in scene in 'Neutral Tones'?

Exam focus

How can I write about mood and tone?

You could use adjectives or adverbs related to the viewpoint or language: e.g. reflective, neutral, bitter, grim or sorrowful.

The speaker presents the death of passion and love as a 'neutral' memory, preserved in shades of 'white' and 'grey' like a photograph, creating distance. However, the death imagery and halting rhythm could suggest a more bitter or sorrowful tone, and the speaker becomes more reflective as they describe how experience has 'shaped' their memories of past love.	Mood words
	Evidence from the language
	How tone/mood develops

Now you try!

Think about other poems in the cluster. Do any share Hardy's bitter tone?

LETTERS FROM YORKSHIRE by Maura Dooley

Dooley's poem explores ideas of physical and emotional distance: two people, whose lives seem separate, nevertheless touch **'souls'** in other ways. From the first-person writing, the speaker could be Dooley herself, but the nature of the relationship is not made explicit.

Shift in second **stanza** from 'he' to 'you', suggesting their closeness

Wintry setting, but with emphasis on warmth and light, rather than the cold

Continuous (-*ing*) verb form emphasises that their lives and routines continue, even when apart

In February, digging his garden, planting potatoes,
he saw the first lapwings return and came
indoors to write to me, his knuckles singing

as they reddened in the warmth.
5   It's not romance, simply how things are.
You out there, in the cold, seeing the seasons

turning, me with my heartful of headlines
feeding words onto a blank screen.
Is your life more real because you dig and sow?

10   You wouldn't say so, breaking ice on a waterbutt,
clearing a path through snow. Still, it's you
who sends me word of that other world

pouring air and light into an envelope. So that
at night, watching the same news in different houses,
15   our souls tap out messages across the icy miles.

Images of communication and writing used throughout

Metaphor of 'singing' rather than 'stinging' highlights pleasure of the cold; it also links to communication vocabulary

Communication: letters aren't just a romantic gesture, they 'feed' love

Enjambment adds to sense of the flow of communication between them

Unexpected word (why not 'head full of'?) could suggest emotional value of her work

Implies that their daily experiences are alien to each other

Juxtaposition of their lives – hers as writer, his active and rural

Metaphor links his words to refreshing nourishment; it could also convey the sense of emotional outpouring

Separation: love survives physical separation when experiences/feelings are still shared

What is the poem's setting?

- The pair in the poem lead **different lives**: she writes; he lives in the countryside, possibly off the land.

- The poem describes their **communication** through his letters, but also creates a sense of a deeper communication and **bond** between them.

What is the poem about?

- **'He'** leaves his **gardening** to write to her about a first sighting of birds. It's never made clear who **'he'** is; the nature of the relationship is **ambiguous**.

- He **writes** to her, but she notes that there's nothing romantic about this: it's one way of **maintaining a relationship**.

- She asks herself if his life is **'more real'** living close to **nature**, before answering herself that he wouldn't think so.

- She emphasises the **physical nature** of his work, but also the fact that it's he who writes to her (even though her job is writing).

- The poem ends with the idea that, even though they live **far apart**, because of the **letters** and shared responses, their **souls** communicate. They know each other well.

Five key things about the language

1. The poem is filled with wintry **imagery** – **'knuckles singing'**, **'ice on a waterbutt'** – but the relationship never *feels* 'cold'.

2. Writing in **free verse** with **enjambment** creates a conversational feel, though the **tercets** form is maintained throughout.

3. Early on, a shift in pronouns from **'he'** to **'you'** brings the male character closer, whilst reminding us of his physical distance from the speaker.

4. Juxtaposition of their daily lives – him **'digging [...] planting'**, her **'feeding words'** onto a screen – emphasises difference in their work.

5. Images of communication throughout – **'write'**, **'feeding words'**, 'breaking ice', **'clearing a path'**, **'sends me word'**, 'pouring', 'tap out' – create a constant sense of their emotional togetherness despite physical separation.

Five key quotations

1. Communication: 'he saw the first lapwings return and came indoors to write to me', ll.2–3: implies closeness to a loved one requires regular communication to share experiences.

2. Realism: 'It's not romance, simply how things are', l.5: letters seem romantic and old-fashioned, but they're also a practical way to connect.

3. Difference: 'Is your life more real because you dig and sow?' l.9: suggests relationships can endure between different people.

4. Importance of love: 'pouring air and light into an envelope', l.13: relationships provide sustenance and life.

5. Closeness: 'our souls tap out messages', l.15: their bond is spiritual in some way, and strong enough to transcend distance.

Note it!

Compare how Dooley presents separation in 'Letters from Yorkshire' with Browning in 'Sonnet 29'. Are there similarities in their emotional responses?

Exam focus

How can I write about the theme of communication in 'Letters from Yorkshire'? AO1 AO2

You can use Dooley's use of imagery to do this.

Images of communication run through the poem. He writes with news, 'pouring air and light into an envelope', sending 'word of that other world'. This suggests that, as long as there is communication in a relationship, it can survive distance. The fact that the letters provide 'air and light' implies that the relationship requires nurturing, like a plant.

- Opening links theme and language
- Examples illustrate point
- Clear explanation of meaning
- Closer analysis

Now you try!

Finish this paragraph about differences, using one of the quotations from the list.

Dooley suggests that having different backgrounds doesn't always matter in a relationship. She states that ....

My progress   Needs more work ☐   Getting there ☐   Sorted! ☐

SPECIAL FOCUS 4: Quotations and references

What do I need to do?

- You need to refer to **words**, **phrases**, **lines** or **verses/stanzas** from the poem in **a clear way** which enables you to **explain** or **interpret** ideas.

How do I do it?

- State the **specific position** of your reference (e.g. *'the final line'*).
- Select the **most appropriate** and **relevant** quotation or reference.
- **Only refer to** what you **need** (don't quote several lines at a time).
- Make sure **direct quotations** are placed in **speech marks**; or if you **paraphrase**, use your **own words**.
- **Embed** any quotations **fluently** in your statements (*'The poet describes his letters as bringing **'air and light'** to her, suggesting they make her feel alive.'*)
- **Explain** meaning, but also **interpret** or **infer** (**suggest** wider **links/ideas**).

Exam focus

How can I use quotations and references effectively? AO1 AO2

Look at this example in which a student comments on the nature of the relationships in 'Letters from Yorkshire'.

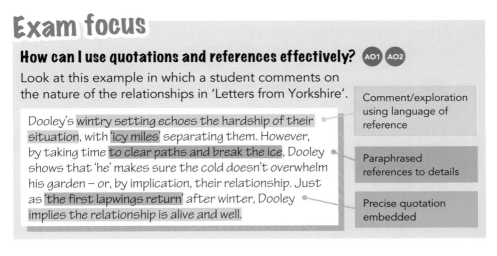

Dooley's wintry setting echoes the hardship of their situation, with 'icy miles' separating them. However, by taking time to clear paths and break the ice, Dooley shows that 'he' makes sure the cold doesn't overwhelm his garden – or, by implication, their relationship. Just as 'the first lapwings return' after winter, Dooley implies the relationship is alive and well.

Comment/exploration using language of reference

Paraphrased references to details

Precise quotation embedded

Now you try!

Use the quotation **'heartful of headlines'** to write a paragraph about conflict between work and love in 'Letters from Yorkshire'.

THE FARMER'S BRIDE by Charlotte Mew

Written in the **voice** of a rural, working man whose young wife has not behaved as he expected, Mew's poem is sympathetic to the difficulties of marriage. Like many of her poems, it reveals sensitivity to unconventional behaviour and lays bare often unspoken themes of sexuality.

'Maid' and 'too young' suggest the farmer understands the cause of the problems in his marriage

Rhymes with long vowels used throughout, suggesting yearning and the dragging of time for the speaker

Fear: the wife fears sexual contact, implied by her antipathy to 'love and me'

Use of nature **imagery** reflects speaker's world

Comparison to a fairy ('fay') emphasises her delicate frame and 'otherworldiness'

Subtle use of **dialect** helps to create a convincing voice

One of the few rhymes with short vowel sounds, said from other speakers – are they less tolerant of the girl's behaviour than her husband?

Simile situates men as hunters and the wife as prey

Male power: shown through their presentation as hunters and jailers

Set apart by the comma, 'fast' (meaning 'tightly closed') implies finality but also safety – from what?

Three summers since I chose a maid,
Too young maybe – but more's to do
At harvest-time than bide and woo.
     When us was wed she turned afraid
5   Of love and me and all things human;
Like the shut of a winter's day
Her smile went out, and 'twasn't a woman—
     More like a little frightened fay.
     One night, in the Fall, she runned away.

10 'Out 'mong the sheep, her be,' they said,
Should properly have been abed;
But sure enough she wasn't there
Lying awake with her wide brown stare.
     So over seven-acre field and up-along across the down
15 We chased her, flying like a hare
Before out lanterns. To Church-Town
     All in a shiver and a scare
We caught her, fetched her home at last
     And turned the key upon her, fast.

20 She does the work about the house
    As well as most, but like a mouse:
        Happy enough to chat and play
        With birds and rabbits and such as they,
        So long as men-folk keep away.
25 'Not near, not near!' her eyes beseech
    When one of us comes within reach.
        The women say that beasts in stall
        Look round like children at her call.
        I've hardly heard her speak at all.

30 Shy as a leveret, swift as he,
    Straight and slight as a young larch tree,
    Sweet as the first wild violets, she,
    To her wild self. But what to me?

    The short days shorten and the oaks are brown,
35   The blue smoke rises to the low grey sky,
    One leaf in the still air falls slowly down,
        A magpie's spotted feathers lie
    On the black earth spread white with rime,
    The berries redden up to Christmas-time.
40   What's Christmas-time without there be
        Some other in the house than we!

        She sleeps up in the attic there
        Alone, poor maid. 'Tis but a stair
    Betwixt us. Oh! my God! the down,
45 The soft young down of her, the brown,
    The brown of her – her eyes, her hair, her hair!

'Beseech' suggests 'begging', only not in words – like a frightened animal

A reminder that the farmer has none, but also suggests she has 'maternal' qualities

End-stopped line highlights his solitude and separation

Repeated comparison of the wife to wild animals, suggesting she cannot be 'tamed'

Pause following his question represents his wife's silence, perhaps

Ominous description of autumn, perhaps echoing his 'shortening' patience

Social and religious convention: represented through references to Christmas and fruitful marriage

Repetition of 'maid' from beginning, coupled with 'poor', emphasises speaker's pity for his wife

Repetition of rhymes, like a moan, hinting at farmer's despair and desire.

Shorter sentences and exclamation reflect increasing emotional turmoil

THE FARMER'S BRIDE by Charlotte Mew

What is the poem's setting?

- The speaker is a farmer in a traditional, rural (probably pre-twentieth century) society, revolving around crops and seasons.
- The farmer lives with his wife, but she fears his company and prefers to spend time with the animals: they sleep apart, and she is still **'a maid'**, i.e. a virgin.

What is the poem about?

- The farmer recounts his marriage and the subsequent **'escape'** of his wife (possibly, Mew hints, after a first sexual experience).
- He and the other men **hunt** down and bring her back. Now, she does the housework, but shuns the company of all men.
- The farmer seems to **respect** his wife's **wildness** and beauty, shown through his **imagery**, but his **longing** bursts through at times.
- As Christmas draws near, he contrasts his situation to those with a house full of **family** and company to celebrate.
- The poem ends with the **image of the young wife, sleeping alone** in the attic, only a stair between them. The speaker breaks down at the thought, and we wonder how long he will be able to **restrain** his **desire** and endure his **loneliness**.

Five key things about the language

1. Nature imagery pervades the poem, reflecting the speaker's world and his sensitivity. It could also suggest that his wife's fear is 'natural'.
2. **Similes** comparing the wife to wild animals emphasise her difference, as well as her fear of 'predatory' men.
3. Rhyming long vowels throughout create a longing **tone**; with **enjambment** and no regular **rhythm** or **stanzas**, we follow the speaker's thoughts.
4. **Narrative** shift from recounting the past, to the present situation and thoughts of Christmas, creates uncertainty in the ending, and a sense of fear.
5. Changing clause lengths, from long to shorter and more disjointed, reflects the speaker's growing agitation and desire.

Five key quotations

1. Incompatibility: 'I chose a maid, / Too young maybe', ll.1–2: different ideas about relationships may make love hard to sustain.
2. Unhappiness: 'Like the shut of a winter's day / Her smile went out', l.6: the speaker feels cut off, as if in darkness.
3. Fear: 'Happy... So long as men-folk keep away', ll.22–4: the wife's terror is of men and the physical power they represent.
4. Loneliness: 'Tis but a stair / Betwixt us', ll.43–4: implies emotional distance may be harder to deal with than physical.
5. Sexual desire: 'The soft young down of her', l.45: here, physical longing is expressed through the sense of touch.

Note it!

Compare how Mew presents unrequited desire in 'The Farmer's Bride' to Shelley's presentation in 'Love's Philosophy'. How does seeing the wife's behaviour affect our response?

Exam focus

How can I write about pre-twentieth century ideas of marriage? (AO3)

You can use the farmer's shift in attitude and focus to explore this.

Although sex was seen as a marital duty at the time, the farmer shows understanding of his wife's fears. He admits she was 'too young maybe' for marriage, and his patience contrasts with the way other people in the poem talk about her unconventional behaviour. However, towards the end, reminded of Christmas and family, the farmer focuses on his own longing, suggesting his understanding won't last forever.

Topic sentence makes clear contextual point linked to marriage

Quotation supports point

Point developed using poem

Shows change of attitude, linking back to original point

Now you try!

Finish this paragraph about desire in the poem, using one of the quotations from the list.

Mew shows the speaker's desire, as he describes ....

My progress　　Needs more work ☐　　Getting there ☐　　Sorted! ☐

WALKING AWAY by Cecil Day Lewis

In this autobiographical poem, subtitled 'For Sean', Day Lewis remembers his son's first day at boarding school. Grappling with the experience of children growing up and away, he explores the 'lessons' he has learned as a parent.

Autumn, 'new term' setting suggests both endings and beginnings

Parenthesis separates main sentence, hinting at distance in time, or a pause for thought

Figurative language used throughout: here, 'wrenched' suggests involuntary separation

It is eighteen years ago, almost to the day –
A sunny day with leaves just turning,
The touch-lines new-ruled – since I watched you play
Your first game of football, then, like a satellite
5 Wrenched from its orbit, go drifting away

Verbs of movement – with a sense of irretrievable loss – echo the title theme, here and below (see 'eddying' and 'loosened', ll.11 and 12)

Behind a scatter of boys. I can see
You walking away from me towards the school
With the pathos of a half-fledged thing set free
Into a wilderness, the gait of one
10 Who finds no path where the path should be.

Metaphor hints at father's fears for his son's vulnerability to danger

Change: the image suggests hesitation faced with an unfamiliar landscape and no clear pathway

That hesitant figure, eddying away
Like a winged seed loosened from its parent stem,
Has something I never quite grasp to convey
About nature's give-and-take – the small, the scorching
15 Ordeals which fire one's irresolute clay.

Double meaning of 'grasp' implies both 'understanding' and 'keeping hold'

Verbs of movement – with a sense of irretrievable loss – echo the title theme

Simile implies that father knows son will take root and grow

Growing up: implies pain, just as, to harden, pottery must pass through fire

32

'Gnaws' suggests that the memory causes ongoing, recurring pain, like hunger

Shifts focus back to present, placing memory in context

Regular rhyme throughout – abaca, etc. – perhaps echoes the way memory keeps circling

'Perhaps' and 'roughly' emphasise reflective **tone**

Parent's perspective: shown as a lesson learned

I have had worse partings, but none that so
Gnaws at my mind still. Perhaps it is roughly
Saying what God alone could perfectly show –
How selfhood begins with a walking away,
20 And love is proved in the letting go.

WALKING AWAY by Cecil Day Lewis

What is the poem's setting?

- The speaker describes watching his son's first game of football, and then how he **walked away** towards school, after the other boys.
- The speaker is Day Lewis himself. He addresses a **now grown-up son**, perhaps moved by the early autumn day that **reminds** him of his son **starting school**.

What is the poem about?

- The poem opens with **change** – leaves turning, **'touch-lines new ruled'**, a first match – and a sense of **new beginnings**.
- The poet tries to describe how it felt to watch his son walk away. Starting with a comparison to a manmade situation (a satellite), he moves to **natural experiences**: a baby animal, a seedling.
- His language suggests his feelings of **anxiety** and **fear** as he entered a new phase of life and **parenthood**, one with **'no path'** for him.
- He seems to feel frustrated at his inability to pinpoint the **mixed sensations** of **'give-and-take'** that the experience held: the pottery image suggests they both undergo a kind of **'growing-up'**.
- The speaker ends with the idea that parents must experience **pain** for their children's sake. The reference to God perhaps recalls religious ideas of **sacrifice**, or the idea that **separation** from parents is natural.

Five key things about the language

1. Use of a personal memory acts as a device from which to explore universal themes.
2. Regular structure of five-line **stanzas** with three rhyming lines and two unrhymed creates a sense of balance.
3. **Enjambment** enhances the sense of flow between memory and the present, with some **end-stopping** helping to shift the **tone**.
4. **Figurative** language throughout echoes the speaker's desire to **'grasp'** ambivalent or complex emotions.
5. Reflective tone hints at pain of experience – **'the scorching ordeals'** – while accepting the recurrent pain of **'letting go'** to find peace in **'love'**.

Five key quotations

1. Fear: 'a half-fledged thing set free / Into a wilderness', ll.8–9: suggests parents' desire to keep children safe.

2. Uncertainty: 'no path where the path should be', l.10: growing up means moving on alone, without parents to guide or map out the way.

3. Acceptance of reality: 'nature's give-and-take', l.14: life encompasses pain and joy, and we can't have one without the other.

4. Independence: 'selfhood begins with a walking away', l.19: a child can only become who they're meant to be by leaving home.

5. Sacrifice: 'love is proved in the letting go', l.20: ironically, real love requires withdrawal of support.

Note it!

Compare how Day Lewis here and Heaney in 'Follower' present the desire to keep hold of a loved one. What differences are there between the parent's and child's perspectives in each case?

Exam focus

How can I write about a parent's perspective in this poem? (AO3)

You can explore the narrative device of memory.

Although he recounts an important day in his son's life, Day Lewis focuses on his own experience of the shared memory. Describing his son as a 'half-fledged thing' emphasises his fear as a parent that his son isn't ready to leave; seeing the world as a 'wilderness' focuses on danger, rather than the excitement a child might feel. However, the viewpoint that the poet presents is one that many readers might recognise.

- Topic sentence makes clear point about the parent's perspective
- Explanation of effects of quotations link back to point
- Considers alternative viewpoint
- Introduces readers' responses

Now you try!

Finish this paragraph about the theme of independence, using one of the quotations from the list.

Day Lewis explores a child's need for independence in a relationship through ....

My progress   Needs more work ☐   Getting there ☐   Sorted! ☐

35

EDEN ROCK by Charles Causley

This poem contains features typical of Causley's poetry such as a feel for landscape (usually Cornish) and religious **imagery**. It may be autobiographical, recalling a childhood memory of his parents, but it also explores universal ideas of death, loneliness and memory.

Use of present tense creates sense of timelessness – memory is preserved

Imprecise language has **connotations** of the after-life, with 'beyond' and 'Eden' reminiscent of Paradise

'Same' and 'still' places the memory at a particular time in his life, emphasising its personal value

They are waiting for me somewhere beyond Eden Rock
My father, twenty-five, in the same suit
of Genuine Irish Tweed, his terrier Jack
Still two years old and trembling at his feet.

Mostly regular use of **quatrains** and **pentameter** of mixed **metres** adds to soothing, almost dream-like **tone**

5   My mother, twenty-three, in a sprigged dress
Drawn at the waist, ribbon in her straw hat,
Has spread the stiff white cloth over the grass
Her hair, the colour of wheat, takes on the light.

Half-rhyme could hint at distance between past and present, or between the speaker and his parents

She pours tea from a Thermos, the milk straight
10   From an old H.P. sauce bottle, a screw
Of paper for a cork; slowly sets out
The same three plates, the tin cups painted blue.

Precise details create an almost photographic image, giving ordinary objects a sense of wonder

Here, 'same' suggests familiarity, as if he recognises the crockery, and the third plate waiting for him

EDEN ROCK by Charles Causley

Recurring vocabulary around 'light' could imply purity or death, or even fading

Almost supernatural imagery, also hinting at visual illusions: is his memory 'true'?

Situates speaker close to parents, but separated by a stream, perhaps symbolising death (e.g. River Styx in Greek mythology)

> The sky whitens as if lit by three suns.
> My mother shades her eyes and looks my way
> 15 Over the drifted stream. My father spins
> A stone along the water. Leisurely,
>
> They beckon to me from the other bank.
> I hear them call, 'See where the stream-path is!
> Crossing is not as hard as you might think.'
>
> 20 I had not thought it would be like this.

Enjambment accentuates the passage of time, like the stream

Connotations of 'the other side', i.e. death, where he can't reach them

Space emphasises his silence – visual **metaphor** for distance

Isolation: emphasised by stand-alone sentence at the end

Parental love: shown in their reassuring words, which might also refer to 'crossing' into death

37

What is the poem's setting?

- The speaker remembers a picnic with his **parents**, who we guess may be dead. We understand his **separation** from his parents as something difficult for him.
- The place, **'Eden Rock'**, creates an atmosphere of light, but Causley himself admitted he had no idea where it was; perhaps it is a symbolic space of **safety** and comfort.

What is the poem about?

- The speaker starts by describing his **father**, before going on to describe his **mother** in the second **stanza**.

- He describes their clothing in some detail, with a **motif** of **light** recurring. The details of the picnic add a sense of period and **familiarity**, with the **'H.P. sauce bottle'** and **'tin cups painted blue'**.
- He describes the sky lightening and his parents' movements, almost as if **time** slows; they are caught, **forever waiting** for him.
- His vocabulary suggests they are happy, as they call to him **'leisurely'** to join them across the **stream**, but also that he is **separated** from them.
- He pauses before speaking – this is not how he'd imagined **'it'**, leaving us uncertain what **'it'** refers to: **death**? Being alone?

Five key things about the language

1. Use of the present tense creates a timeless feel, suggesting his parents live on in memory.
2. Motifs of light possess **connotations** of happiness, as well as the afterlife – light at the end of the tunnel.
3. Use of the stream may be both literal and **figurative**, with streams as boundaries between life and death, or a stream of thought and memory.
4. Precise details imply clear recollection or, perhaps, an old photograph; they emphasise the importance of ordinary things to our sense of the past.
5. Half-rhymes are subtle, but could suggest a dislocation between memory and reality, blurring lines between death and life.

Five key quotations

1. **Family:** 'They are waiting for me somewhere …', l.1: we are tied to family even when separated.
2. **Familiarity:** 'Her hair, the colour of wheat, takes on the light', l.8: familiar things can become beautiful from a distance.
3. **Comfort:** 'slowly sets out the same three plates', l.12: family life may be ordinary, but it can be comforting in its unchanging routines.
4. **Parental love:** 'Crossing is not as hard as you might think', l.19: parents reassure children when they show fear.
5. **Loss:** 'I had not thought it would be like this', l.20: it is hard to imagine life without parents who have been with you since birth.

Note it!

Compare how Causley explores independence from parents with Duffy's presentation of her mother in 'Before You Were Mine'. How do they present distance and love?

Exam focus

How can I write about the death of loved ones in the poem? AO1 AO2

You can use Causley's opening and ending to explore this.

In the first line the speaker reveals his dead parents are 'waiting for [him] somewhere …'. The phrase suggests he doesn't know where exactly, but trusts they're there for him, implying a sense of faith. The light imagery that Causley uses throughout also seems to reflect the comfort of religious ideas that he'll see them again. However, in the final line, the speaker leaves us with a sudden feeling of loneliness: 'I had not thought it would be like this.'

- Relevant reference linked to task
- Explanation developed
- Adds detail to support point
- Shows contrasting tone of the end

Now you try!

Finish this paragraph about parental love, using one of the quotations from the list.

Causley presents parental love, by ....

FOLLOWER by Seamus Heaney

In this poem, Heaney evokes a childhood in rural Ireland very like his own – his father was a cattle-dealer – as he explores the complexity of the parent–child relationship through an everyday, farming task.

Shifts focus from father to son: 'my father', then 'I' halfway through

Like Atlas carrying the globe on his shoulders, the father is strong and giantlike

Sea imagery recurs throughout, hinting at father's graceful – and old-fashioned? – power, like a galleon

My father worked with a horse-plough,
His shoulders globed like a full sail strung
Between the shafts and the furrow.
The horse strained at his clicking tongue.

5   An expert. He would set the wing
And fit the bright steel-pointed sock.
The sod rolled over without breaking.
At the headrig, with a single pluck

Of reins, the sweating team turned round
10   And back into the land. His eye
Narrowed and angled at the ground,
Mapping the furrow exactly.

I stumbled in his hob-nailed wake,
Fell sometimes on the polished sod;
15   Sometimes he rode me on his back
Dipping and rising to his plod.

Suggests intuitive power over animals

Short statement suggests no one would argue with his judgement

Rural terminology emphasises father's 'expertise'

Enjambment across **stanza** break echoes and emphasises smoothness of father's movements

Verbs suggest almost mechanical precision of his eye, with no instruments to help

Juxtaposition suggests that father's care makes even dirt valuable

Steady support: symbolised by image of piggyback and 'plod'

Contrast between father's grace and son's clumsiness – the term is repeated in final stanza, to show reversal of roles

Recalls father's action, but perhaps also another mythical giant, one-eyed Cyclops

Child's perspective – 'I want to be a ...' – shown through **tone** of admiration

Tetrameter and abab rhyme (half- and full-rhymes) echoes father's steady pace

> I wanted to grow up and plough,
> To close one eye, stiffen my arm.
> All I ever did was follow
> 20 In his broad shadow round the farm.
>
> I was a nuisance, tripping, falling,
> Yapping always. But today
> It is my father who keeps stumbling
> Behind me, and will not go away.

Inadequacy: the speaker's tone hints he is measuring himself against his father

Verbs underline the idea of being 'a nuisance'

Title of poem suggests father was almost godlike to his young son, his disciple – an idea overturned here

Pause before this suggests speaker's sense of irritation, and also guilt that his father showed more patience than he can now

Reversal of roles: the parent becomes dependent on the child with age

41

What is the poem's setting?

- Heaney's rich yet precise vocabulary creates a vivid picture of a **rural world** losing ground to 'modern Ireland'.
- The ploughing image could represent each individual's **struggle** to 'plough their own furrow', or the way in which we are 'yoked' to our **past** even as we try to move forward.

What is the poem about?

- The first three **stanzas** focus on the father's **'expert'** strength and skill, describing his actions in loving detail.
- The evocative description echoes his father's own focus and **commitment** to **'the land'** with **admiration** on the speaker's part.
- The speaker shifts the focus to his child self, who 'stumbled' behind, getting in the way; the father responds with **patience**, allowing the child to ride on his back.

- The speaker wished to **follow** in his father's footsteps as a child and work the horse-plough, perhaps suggesting he later changed his mind.
- In the final stanza, the speaker moves to the present, revealing the weight of things that 'will not go away': the **burden** of an ageing dependent, **memories** of his father and of his own childhood, and the **complex emotions** of **adulthood**.

Five key things about the language

1. **Imagery**, particularly sea and ship imagery, is used to emphasise the father's strength, giving the work a kind of glamour in a child's eyes.
2. Specialist terminology evokes skill and rural knowledge (perhaps contrasting with Heaney's own 'bookish' work as a university lecturer and writer).
3. Regular stanza and line length, with a regular rhyme scheme, echo the father's steady plod through the fields.
4. The descriptive focus shifts from father to son halfway through, **foreshadowing** the reversal that is revealed in the final stanza.
5. Verb repetition (**'stumble'** / **'stumbling'**) highlights both similarities and differences between father and son.

Five key quotations

1. Respect: 'An expert', l.5: the poet shows admiration for his father's skill, as something separate from their relationship.

2. Devotion: 'I stumbled in his hob-nailed wake', l.13: implies a struggle to keep up with his father's dogged stride.

3. Parental support: 'he rode me on his back', l.15: suggesting parents carry their children, literally and **metaphorically**.

4. Ambivalence: 'his broad shadow', l.20: a shadow shields from the heat, but also blocks out light.

5. Reversal of roles: 'today / It is my father who keeps stumbling / Behind me', ll.22–4: he has moved on from this rural world, yet the figure of his father shadows him (literally or figuratively).

Note it!

Compare Heaney's child's perspective with that of Waterhouse in 'Climbing My Grandfather'. How are familiar landscapes used to create a sense of love?

Exam focus

How can I write about language effects in this poem? (AO2)

You can use Heaney's use of detail to explore this.

Heaney uses detail to imply many emotions in a single line: the speaker recalls how he 'stumbled' after his father, suggesting eagerness to keep up, but also how the heavy soil slowed him down. This is contrasted to his father's smooth, sailing-ship 'wake', as he glides along. The speaker remembers his 'hob-nailed' boots, suggesting how a small child's gaze is firmly fixed on their parent, unable to see higher or further than immediate details.

- Topic sentence introduces focus
- Detailed examination of effects
- Further language effects explored
- Effects linked to wider perspectives

Now you try!

Finish this paragraph about parental support, using one of the quotations from the list.

Heaney shows how parents support their children, by ....

My progress   Needs more work ☐   Getting there ☐   Sorted! ☐   **43**

MOTHER, ANY DISTANCE by Simon Armitage

This poem is from Armitage's third poetry collection, *A Book of Matches*, published in 1993. Addressing his mother, who has come to help him measure rooms for his new house, he explores ideas around their changing relationship.

Present tense creates movement and immediacy, as if we are following the characters

Direct address emphasises the bond, stressing that *everyone* needs help to stretch a tape further than their own arm span

Semantic field of space – physical and **metaphorical** – echoes theme of moving out

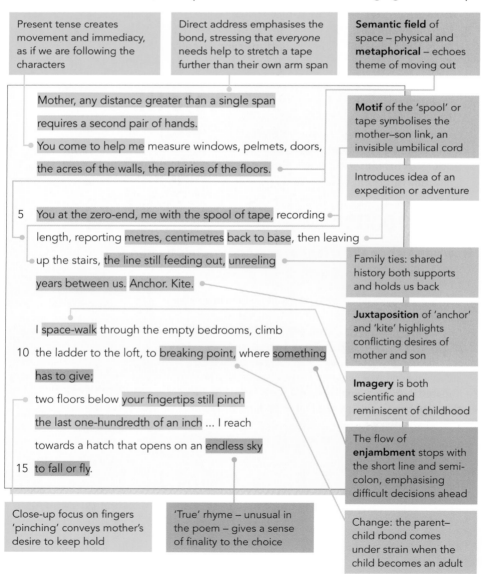

Mother, any distance greater than a single span

requires a second pair of hands.

You come to help me measure windows, pelmets, doors,

the acres of the walls, the prairies of the floors.

5   You at the zero-end, me with the spool of tape, recording

length, reporting metres, centimetres back to base, then leaving

up the stairs, the line still feeding out, unreeling

years between us. Anchor. Kite.

I space-walk through the empty bedrooms, climb

10   the ladder to the loft, to breaking point, where something

has to give;

two floors below your fingertips still pinch

the last one-hundredth of an inch ... I reach

towards a hatch that opens on an endless sky

15   to fall or fly.

Motif of the 'spool' or tape symbolises the mother–son link, an invisible umbilical cord

Introduces idea of an expedition or adventure

Family ties: shared history both supports and holds us back

Juxtaposition of 'anchor' and 'kite' highlights conflicting desires of mother and son

Imagery is both scientific and reminiscent of childhood

The flow of **enjambment** stops with the short line and semi-colon, emphasising difficult decisions ahead

Close-up focus on fingers 'pinching' conveys mother's desire to keep hold

'True' rhyme – unusual in the poem – gives a sense of finality to the choice

Change: the parent–child rbond comes under strain when the child becomes an adult

What is the poem's setting?

- The poem describes a young man as he **prepares to move** into a new house, helped by his mother.
- From the description, the house could be anywhere and seems empty, perhaps representing the **universality** of the experience that Armitage explores.

What is the poem about?

- The speaker describes his mother helping him before he moves into a new house; they are measuring rooms together.
- The theme **of relationships** is explored as the mother and son explore the house, showing their **different attitudes to change**.
- As they move apart, the tape measure they hold between them extends: the **'distance'** of the title is therefore both literal – moving into a new home – and metaphorical – the **mental and emotional distance** such a move can entail.

- The speaker climbs to the loft, reaching for the window, symbolising **freedom**, while his mother maintains a tight grip on her end of the tape measure.
- With the final line, we are left to wonder how the speaker will **cope** with the new distance – to use different **imagery**, will he **'sink'** or **'swim'**?

Five key things about the language

1. Armitage uses the **extended metaphor** of the tape measure throughout the poem, perhaps echoing the umbilical cord that links mother and child.
2. A semantic field of space and distance emphasises themes of freedom and security, love and letting go.
3. **Enjambment** leads us to follow the speaker as if through the rooms of the house.
4. Half-rhymes create a sense of things not quite matching – perhaps the speaker's and his mother's views? – and emphasises the 'true' strong rhymes in lines 3 and 4, and 14 and 15.
5. The speaker's use of pronouns – **'you'**, **'me'**, and one **'us'** – shows how he tries to imagine the different perspectives of both figures in the scene.

Five key quotations

1. Exploration: 'the acres of the walls, the prairies of the floors,' l.4: **metaphors** suggest freedom and space, a child's eye view of the rooms.

2. Support: 'back to base,' l.6: parents are there at the start of our journey: they stay while children move on.

3. Relationships: 'unreeling / years between us', ll.7–8: the verb suggests how shared memories hold mother and son together.

4. Ambiguity: 'Anchor. Kite', l.8: the images suggest both support and restriction. An anchor (for kite or ship) holds an object secure/back.

5. Setting free: 'to breaking point, where something / has to give,' ll.10–11: the mother must change and let her son forge his own life, or risk damaging their relationship.

Note it!

Compare how Armitage presents the mother's perspective to Day Lewis's speaker in 'Walking Away'. Do they express similar thoughts?

Exam focus

How can I write about imagery in the poem? (AO2)

You can use it to show how Armitage explores parent–child relationships.

Armitage's use of space imagery suggests that, for the child, moving away is a momentous step. While the speaker 'space-walks' through the house like an astronaut, his mother remains back at the 'base'; they are connected by a 'line'. However, the imagery also reminds us that, while his mother may hold him back, she also supports him, highlighting the delicate balance of parent–child relationships.

- Topic sentence links language and effect
- Precise references support the point
- Signals an alternative interpretation
- Links back to ideas about theme

Now you try!

Finish this paragraph about freedom, using one of the quotations from the list.

The poet suggests that it is important for parents to let their children explore. This is presented through ....

My progress   Needs more work ☐   Getting there ☐   Sorted! ☐

SPECIAL FOCUS 5: Comparing poems

What do I need to do?

- In **Section B** of your exam paper, you will need to comment on the ways a **given poem** from the cluster, and one **of your own choice** from the cluster, explore a **specific issue** or **relationship**.

How do I do it?

- **Select** your **choice of poem** quickly but carefully based on the **question**.
- **Annotate** the given poem, and **link** your notes on your chosen poem.
- **Decide** on the **aspects** you are going **to compare**, and **structure** your response based on these aspects.
- **Decide** whether you will tackle **one poem** first, **then the other** – or **compare/contrast** ideas as **you go along**.
- **Make clear** what aspect you are tackling at the **start of each paragraph**.
- Use **comparative** and **contrasting** connective words and phrases (e.g. 'even though', 'however', etc.). **Synthesise** ideas to give **an overview** of aspects of the two poems (*'Both poems use violent imagery ...'*).

Exam focus

How can I compare two poems? AO1

Look at this example.

> Both speakers imagine how the parent might feel about change. Armitage's speaker sees his mother 'pinching the last inch' of time together, suggesting a need to cling tightly to her son. Duffy's speaker, however, suggests how her own 'loud, possessive yell' has chased away the 'tomorrows' her mother might have had. This suggests how children hold back parents, whereas Armitage explores how parents hold back children.

- Both poems linked through perspective
- Idea developed with references
- Comparative connectives
- Final sentence summarises ideas

Now you try!

Write a further paragraph comparing how the two poets use imagery to explore the theme of change.

BEFORE YOU WERE MINE by Carol Ann Duffy

Duffy has described this poem to her mother as 'entirely autobiographical'. It is full of vivid, personal detail, but it also explores universal themes of parenthood. Duffy imagines her mother as a girl, implicitly considering how her own birth has changed and shaped her mother's life.

Reminders given throughout the poem to suggest how far the mother has come from her past

Loud verb creates an image of teenage girls having fun

Reference to famous photo of Marilyn Monroe standing over subway vent conjures the glamour her mother longed for

Short sentence reminds us of reality among the 'dreams'

Imagery hints at excitement: 'thousand eyes' suggests flirting and disco-balls, 'fizzy' connotes champagne

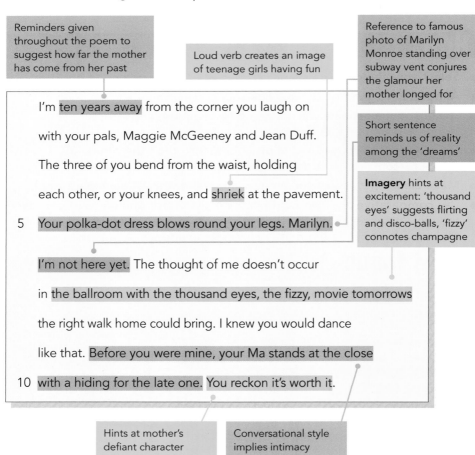

I'm ten years away from the corner you laugh on

with your pals, Maggie McGeeney and Jean Duff.

The three of you bend from the waist, holding

each other, or your knees, and shriek at the pavement.

5　Your polka-dot dress blows round your legs. Marilyn.

I'm not here yet. The thought of me doesn't occur

in the ballroom with the thousand eyes, the fizzy, movie tomorrows

the right walk home could bring. I knew you would dance

like that. Before you were mine, your Ma stands at the close

10　with a hiding for the late one. You reckon it's worth it.

Hints at mother's defiant character

Conversational style implies intimacy

Sensory **imagery** evokes complex nature of memory

Questions suggest daughter's sympathy for her mother

'Relics' suggests almost religious devotion for the red shoes, symbolising daring

The decade ahead of my loud, possessive yell was the best one, eh?

I remember my hands in those high-heeled red shoes, relics,

and now your ghost clatters toward me over George Square

till I see you, clear as scent, under the tree,

15 with its lights, and whose small bites on your neck, sweetheart?

Cha cha cha! You'd teach me the steps on the way home from Mass,

stamping stars from the wrong pavement. Even then

I wanted the bold girl winking in Portobello, somewhere

in Scotland, before I was born. That glamorous love lasts

20 where you sparkle and waltz and laugh before you were mine.

Repetition of 'before' from title and line 9 reminds us this is all past

Present tense use of joyful verbs implies she still sees this in her mother

Possessive love: 'mine' conveys child's 'ownership' of her mother

Worship: child's idolisation of a parent is evoked in the idea of 'glamorous' love

Reference to 1950s dance craze and Hollywood Walk of Fame recalls glamour, and freedom of post-war years

BEFORE YOU WERE MINE by Carol Ann Duffy

What is the poem's setting?

- Duffy is the speaker here, describing her mother as a young woman in Glasgow, based on her mother's **anecdotes**.
- The poem brings to life the decade before Duffy's birth, the mid-1940s to 1950s, when the speaker's mother still lived with her own mother.

What is the poem about?

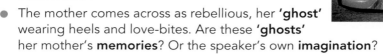

- Directly addressing her mother, the speaker pictures her laughing on the street with 'pals', mixing personal **anecdote** with popular images.
- The speaker repeats that she's **'not here yet'**, picturing a time when her mother hasn't even imagined **being a mother**. Instead, the speaker describes a girl's **dreams** of **'fizzy, movie tomorrows'**.
- The mother comes across as rebellious, her **'ghost'** wearing heels and love-bites. Are these **'ghosts'** her mother's **memories**? Or the speaker's own **imagination**?
- In the final **stanza**, Duffy shifts the focus to her own **childhood**, with her mother mischievously teaching her dance-steps coming home from church.
- There is a sense of **worship** for this **'glamorous'** figure, as we sense how the speaker **regrets** never knowing the girl who was to become her mother.

Five key things about the language

1. **Narrative** focus plays with our sense of time by describing events that the speaker can't have actually seen.
2. Conversational **tone** – **'eh?'**, **'a hiding'**, **'your Ma'** – creates a sense of intimacy and reflects the mother's Scottish background.
3. Repetition of time phrases – 'Before You Were Mine' – suggests the speaker is now the age her mother was in the poem, reminding us the mother is now old, or even dead.
4. **'Glamorous' imagery** – **'Marilyn'**, red heels – reflects a young woman's aspirations, implying that 'unglamorous' responsibility chases them away.
5. Vivid sensory vocabulary – **'fizzy'**, **'clatters'**, **'sparkle'** – reflects mother's liveliness, showing how the child is attracted to this lost side of her mother.

Five key quotations

1. Romance: 'The thought of me doesn't occur', l.6: the young, yet-to-be mother dreams of romantic love, not considering the parental responsibility this may lead to.

2. Dreams/hopes: 'fizzy, movie tomorrows', l.7: her teenage dreams are filled with excitement and possibility.

3. Child's perspective: 'Before you were mine', l.9: suggests children see parents as 'theirs', forgetting they have or had lives independent of them.

4. Possessive love: 'my loud, possessive yell', l.11: children demand parents' attention and time from the moment they are born.

5. Devotion: 'That glamorous love', l.19: the daughter's love is a kind of romantic hero-worship.

Note it!

Compare how Duffy explores ideas about possessive parental love here to Day Lewis in 'Walking Away'. What are the similarities between a child's and parent's perspectives in these poems?

Exam focus

How can I write about loss in this poem? AO1 AO2

You can use Duffy's vocabulary to explore this.

> Duffy hints at a lost girlhood through her vocabulary. She presents her mother dreaming of 'fizzy, movie tomorrows' and 'ballrooms' that 'sparkle', implying that her mother lost everything 'glamorous' when she became a parent: 'fizzy' things have gone 'flat'. Yet Duffy also explores the way a child longs for a parent to be fun-loving and childlike, suggesting she herself has lost 'the bold girl winking in Portobello'.

- Topic sentence links task to language
- Explores relevant quotations
- Signals a second interpretation linked to developed idea
- Links second idea back to task

Now you try!

Finish this paragraph about a child's love, using one of the quotations from the list:

Carol Ann Duffy explores ideas of possessive love through . . . .

WINTER SWANS by Owen Sheers

In this poem, Sheers implicitly compares a couple struggling in their relationship to a pair of swans who **'mate for life'**. As with other poems in his first collection, *Skirrid Hill*, he uses the natural world and the Welsh landscape to explore human relationships.

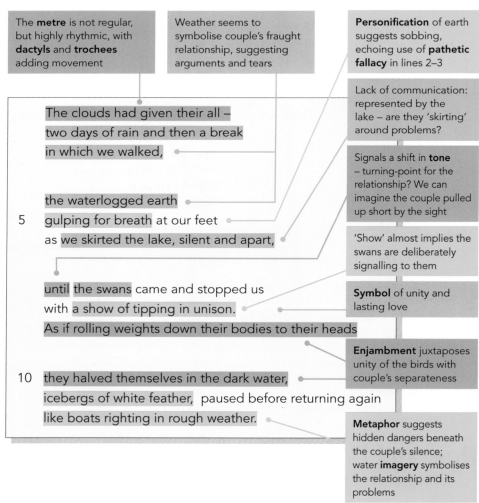

The **metre** is not regular, but highly rhythmic, with **dactyls** and **trochees** adding movement

Weather seems to symbolise couple's fraught relationship, suggesting arguments and tears

Personification of earth suggests sobbing, echoing use of **pathetic fallacy** in lines 2–3

Lack of communication: represented by the lake – are they 'skirting' around problems?

Signals a shift in **tone** – turning-point for the relationship? We can imagine the couple pulled up short by the sight

'Show' almost implies the swans are deliberately signalling to them

Symbol of unity and lasting love

Enjambment juxtaposes unity of the birds with couple's separateness

Metaphor suggests hidden dangers beneath the couple's silence; water **imagery** symbolises the relationship and its problems

The clouds had given their all –
two days of rain and then a break
in which we walked,

the waterlogged earth
5 gulping for breath at our feet
as we skirted the lake, silent and apart,

until the swans came and stopped us
with a show of tipping in unison.
As if rolling weights down their bodies to their heads

10 they halved themselves in the dark water,
icebergs of white feather, paused before returning again
like boats righting in rough weather.

Suggestive of purity and whiteness, but also perhaps fragility: will the relationship endure?

Resilience: implicit comparison to swans makes us question the durability of human relationships

'They mate for life' you said as they left,
porcelain over the stilling water. I didn't reply
15 but as we moved on through the afternoon light,

Sibilance echoes sound of the water on stones

slow-stepping in the lake's shingle and sand,
I noticed our hands, that had, somehow,
swum the distance between us

Hands represent the couple's relationship, linked back to swans with 'swum'

and folded, one over the other,
20 like a pair of wings settling after flight.

Ends differently: two-line stanza may symbolise couple moving together like the 'pair' of swans

53

WINTER SWANS by Owen Sheers

What is the poem's setting?

- A couple having **difficulties** in their relationship walk around a lake after **'two days of rain'**. Much of Sheers's poetry is set around the Welsh countryside where he grew up.
- The lake sets the couple in natural **isolation**, but could also represent problems beneath the surface, or the way we must 'navigate' **problems in love**.

What is the poem about?

- The poem opens with rain, which has kept the couple inside; in **'a break'**, they have come outside.
- The sodden ground sucks at their feet as they walk, **'silent and apart'**, suggesting **distance** between them, and heaviness like mud.
- Suddenly, they see **two swans** and stop to watch their sinuous movements, pale on the dark lake, suggesting grace and **joy**.
- The partner comments that swans **'mate for life'** as they watch the birds swim away; the speaker says nothing, but notes the afternoon **'light'**, and that they are now holding hands **'somehow'**.
- Their hands symbolise a **bridge** between them, linking to the swans in the idea of **'wings'**: the couple may weather their difficulties after all. Could the swans also remind us it is hard work keeping a relationship 'afloat'?

Five key things about the language

1. Irregular but lilting **rhythm** generates movement, perhaps echoing the swans' 'dance', or the ups-and-downs of a relationship.
2. **Enjambment** creates a smooth flow of images, again mirroring the birds' grace.
3. Nature **imagery** permeates the poem, with pathetic fallacy in the weather echoing the couple's relationship.
4. Symbolic language – the lake, the swans, the hands – creates a deeper layer of meaning so that, while autobiographical, the poem explores universal experience.
5. Structurally, the final two-line **stanza**, after previous **tercets**, recalls a **sonnet's rhyming couplet** with a sense of togetherness and resolution.

Five key quotations

1. **Communication:** 'we skirted the lake, silent and apart', l.6: unspoken or spoken problems can separate a couple. Calm may be an illusion.
2. **Unity:** 'tipping in unison', l.8: swans represent an idea of unity and togetherness in a relationship.
3. **Endurance:** 'like boats righting in rough weather', l.12: the relationship may survive, with some hard work.
4. **Romantic ideals:** 'They mate for life', l.13: lasting monogamy is an ideal that we are drawn to and try to find in nature.
5. **Separation:** 'our hands, that had, somehow, swum the distance between us', ll.17–18: emotional distance is here bridged by physical closeness.

Note it!

Compare how Sheers explores problems in a relationship here with Hardy in 'Neutral Tones'. How do they use nature to create atmosphere and symbolic meanings?

Exam focus

How can I write about effects of language in the poem? (AO2)

You can use Sheers's swan symbolism to explore this.

> Sheers's swan imagery symbolises an ideal of an effortlessly harmonious relationship, as the swans move calm as 'icebergs' across the water; the idea that swans 'mate for life' creates an impression that such a relationship is natural, yet we could also consider the swans' legs working fast beneath the surface to remember that maintaining a relationship may be hard work.

Opening clearly links language and ideas

Relevant quotations support point

Clear explanation of effect

Develops alternative layers of meaning

Now you try!

Finish this paragraph about language effects, using one of the quotations from the list.

Sheers explores ideas about communication in a relationship by ....

SINGH SONG! by Daljit Nagra

Daljit Nagra explores immigrant experiences in modern Britain in this poem, using a Punjabi-influenced English sometimes called 'Punglish'. Here, the speaker is torn between his duties running his father's shop and the pleasure he takes in spending time with his new bride.

I run just one ov my daddy's shops
from 9 o'clock to 9 o'clock
and he vunt me not to hav a break
but ven nobody in, I do di lock –

5 cos up di stairs is my newly bride
vee share in chapatti
vee share in di chutney
after vee hav made luv
like vee rowing through Putney –

10 Ven I return vid my pinnie untied
di shoppers always point and cry:
Hey Singh, ver yoo bin?
Yor lemons are limes
yor bananas are plantain,
15 *dis dirty little floor need a little bit of mop*
in di worst Indian shop
on di whole Indian road –

Above my head high heel tap di ground
as my vife on di web is playing wid di mouse
20 ven she netting two cat on her Sikh lover site
she book dem for di meat at di cheese ov her price –

my bride
    she effing at my mum
    in all di colours of Punjabi
25   den stumble like a drunk
    making fun at my daddy

my bride
    tiny eyes ov a gun
    and di tummy ov a teddy

Contrast hints at conflict between duty (daddy) and love (bride)

Speaker mixes Punjabi and English expressions to create a distinctive voice

Rhyme and rhythm enhance joyful feel and lend a comic tone

Sexual imagery (see l.35, or fourth stanza) hints at energetic love life

Use of a refrain (see ll.35) evokes repetitiveness of daily life, eroding romance with reality

Customers' voices show prejudiced attitudes towards immigrant communities in Britain

Ambiguous language suggests wife's modern streak running an online dating agency

Conflict: the speaker has divided loyalties

Repetition of 'bride' emphasises speaker's love

Contrasting imagery: she may be tough but he finds her adorable

Mixed national dress echoes conflict – cultural, generational – that the speaker feels

His wife helps to catch teenage thieves

'Tickle' recalls playful imagery about sex, suggesting fun

30   my bride
        she hav a red crew cut
        and she wear a Tartan sari
        a donkey jacket and some pumps
        on di squeak ov di girls dat are pinching my sweeties –

35   Ven I return from di tickle ov my bride
     di shoppers always point and cry:
     Hey Singh, ver yoo bin?
     Di milk is out ov date
     and di bread is alvays stale,
40   *di tings yoo hav on offer yoo hav never got in stock*
     in di worst Indian shop
     on di whole Indian road –

     Late in di midnight hour
     ven yoo shoppers are wrap up quiet
45   ven di precinct is concrete-cool
     vee cum down whispering stairs
     and sit on my silver stool,
     from behind di chocolate bars
     vee stare past di half-price window signs
50   at di beaches ov di UK in di brightey moon –

     from di stool each night she say,
          How much do yoo charge for dat moon baby?

     from di stool each night I say,
          Is half di cost ov yoo baby,

55   from di stool each night she say,
          How much does dat come to baby?

     from di stool each night I say,
          Is priceless baby –

Night-time shifts the **mood** to more reflective and personal, without 'yoo shoppers', i.e. us?

Semantic field of evening quiet contrasts to daytime noise and colour, suggesting peace

Pun on 'bars' suggests imprisonment: does the speaker feel trapped?

Symbol of moon representing romance or far-fetched dreams, or perhaps change

Affectionate term holds ideas of protection; both use it, suggesting their closeness

Paired lines reflect the couple's closeness

Power of love: love transcends money (both his daddy's shop and wife's business)

What is the poem's setting?

- The speaker – second-generation British Sikh, like Nagra himself – runs one of his **'daddy's shops'**, living above it with his **'newly bride'**.

- The **'Indian shop'** setting draws attention to **stereotypical views**, hinting at racist attitudes but also sending up **cultural norms**: perhaps the speaker has disappointed his parents by not having his own shops.

What is the poem about?

- The speaker opens with his father's **expectations** of work, which he fails to fulfil by sneaking off for sex with his new wife.

- The focus shifts to customer complaints, and the racist comments that the speaker faces; he is acutely aware of his wife above, running her online Sikh dating agency.

- The central part focuses on the bride and how her ways **conflict** with those of his parents, for whom she shows little **respect**. Her **'Tartan sari'** represents her unconventional outlook.

- The speaker returns to the **demands** of customers via the girls stealing his sweets, again highlighting the lack of respect he feels at work.

- The poem ends with the shop closed, when his wife emerges. They sit together in the quiet, **dreaming** of holidays, reassuring each other of their love.

Five key things about the language

1. Distinctive 'voice' combines Punjabi inflections and syntax with English vocabulary to echo speaker's many conflicts.

2. **Imagery** similarly combines English and Punjabi **symbols** to show speaker's – and even more so, his wife's – mixed heritage.

3. The rhyme and rhythmic lines emphasise the language, hinting at the speaker's positive attitude (as well as critiquing racist jokes about 'sing-song' accents).

4. Repetition emphasises speaker's recurring thoughts, as well as the power of his love.

5. Openly sexual imagery suggests speaker's passion and joy in his relationship, and the fact this is a 'modern' marriage.

Five key quotations

1. Duty: 'he vunt me not to hav a break', l.3: suggests how family and romantic love pull the speaker in different directions.

2. Marriage: 'her Sikh lover site', l.20: suggesting his wife values choice in marriage, rather than traditional matchmaking.

3. Attraction: 'tiny eyes ov a gun / and di tummy ov a teddy', ll.28–9: the imagery here illustrates the subjective nature of attraction.

4. Sexual love: 'di tickle ov my bride', l.35: to the speaker, sex and romance are fun, as well as deeply felt.

5. Value of love: 'Is priceless baby', l.58: echoes romantic clichés: you can't buy love; love is its own reward.

Note it!

Compare how Nagra's speaker reveals ideas about the effect of social expectation on love to Mew's in 'The Farmer's Bride'. Despite differences in time and culture, are there similarities?

Exam focus

How can I write about conflicting ideas of love? AO1 AO3

You can use Nagra's characters to explore this.

> Nagra's speaker seems delighted with his 'newly bride', but she represents new ideas of which his parents disapprove. She sees marriage as a choice, running a 'Sikh lover site', which may conflict with the tradition of arranged marriage. With her 'effing' and own business, she is probably not the daughter-in-law the speaker's parents dreamed of to help run the shop, and Nagra uses her to illustrate conflict between different generations.

Topic sentence links poem and task

Relevant quotations in support

Explanation linked to context

Links back to task

Now you try!

Finish this paragraph about the value of love. Use one of the quotations from the list.

Nagra's speaker presents the romantic idea that love is worth more than anything by

....

CLIMBING MY GRANDFATHER
by Andrew Waterhouse

Waterhouse's poetry often draws upon his deeply-felt environmentalism, and this poem is no different, using landscape **imagery** to create an impression of a man of great stature, both literally and **figuratively**.

Enjambment appears here for the first time creating the smooth flow of the 'climb'

Refers to 'climbing' of title – the **metaphor** could refer to the idea of 'scaling' memories

The poem is written in **free verse**, and the idea of 'free climbing' puns on this

I decide to do it free, without a rope or net.
First, the old brogues, dusty and cracked;
an easy scramble onto his trousers,
pushing into the weave, trying to get a grip.

5   By the overhanging shirt I change
Direction, traverse along his belt
to an earth-stained hand. The nails
are splintered and give good purchase,
the skin of his finger is smooth and thick

10   like warm ice. On his arm I discover
the glassy ridge of a scar, place my feet
gently in the old stitches and move on.
At his still firm shoulder, I rest for a while
in the shade, not looking down,

15   for climbing has its dangers, then pull
myself up the loose skin of his neck
to a smiling mouth to drink among teeth.
Refreshed, I cross the screed cheek,
to stare into his brown eyes, watch a pupil

20   slowly open and close. Then up over
the forehead, the wrinkles well-spaced
and easy, to his thick hair (soft and white
at this altitude), reaching for the summit,
where gasping for breath I can only lie

25   watching clouds and birds circle,
feeling his heat, knowing
the slow pulse of his good heart.

Semantic field of climbing, with active verbs suggesting effort, develops the metaphor

Details suggest a life of hard work

Startling **paradox** captures feel of well-worn skin (from work)

'Rest' gives a pause midway in the poem, conveying that the grandfather provides support

Remembrance: recalling a loved one may raise painful memories or a sense of loss

Implies that he's filled up with more memories, or that memories themselves 'refresh' us

Description hints at happy old age

Admiration: we try to follow grandparents

Single-syllable words echo heartbeat, implying love

What is the poem's setting?

- The speaker uses a metaphor of **climbing**, so that his grandfather is a 'mountain'. This may reflect Waterhouse's childhood in a northern landscape and subsequent environmentalism.
- The poem feels autobiographical, with the poet writing as grandson – the detail suggests **intimate knowledge** and love.

What is the poem about?

- The speaker decides to climb **'free'**, unsupported by ropes, implying he's embarking on a dangerous **adventure**. Why? Is it hard to **remember**?
- The ascent starts easily with the dusty shoes and trousers, becoming more difficult the higher the speaker gets. His grandfather seems almost giant-sized.
- As he climbs, he uses his grandfather's physical features – a scar, his neck skin – to move higher, suggesting the **support** his grandfather provides (provided?) for him.
- He has to stop for a rest several times – at his grandfather's shoulder, his mouth – suggesting the task is hard work and tiring.
- Finally, he reaches **'the summit'** and, too breathless to do more, lies and gazes at the sky, feeling his grandfather's **warmth** beneath him.

Five key things about the language

1. The climbing metaphor recalls a child's excitement at clambering on a much-loved grandparent, as well as suggesting ideas of 'measuring up' to a hero-figure.
2. Vivid and varied verbs linked to climbing suggest that remembering is hard work but also absorbing and rewarding.
3. **Free verse** echoes 'free climbing', creating an idea that he is following the old man's contours, trying to get a measure of his grandfather.

4. Enjambment enhances the feel of smooth and steady climbing.
5. Descriptions of the 'landscape' of the old man imply his stature – a 'mountain' of a man – but they all connote warmth and softness, despite the crags and **'wrinkles'** of age and work.

Five key quotations

1. Exploration: **'I decide to do it free, without a rope or net'**, l.1: could suggest there are no rules or careful plans for memories – they can lead us anywhere.
2. Understanding: **'trying to get a grip'**, l.4: suggests importance of empathy when approaching the past.
3. Support: **'his still firm shoulder'**, l.13: older family members may provide support, physical or emotional, when we are struggling.
4. Respect: **'reaching for the summit'**, l.23: we look up to older family at times, seeing them as distant or different to us.
5. Memory: **'feeling his heat'**, l.26: memory brings back love, and perhaps a sense of understanding and peace.

Note it!

Compare how Waterhouse explores distance in family relationships to Causley in 'Eden Rock'. How far do you think these poems relate to death?

Exam focus

How can I write about memory in this poem?

You can use Waterhouse's use of free verse to explore this.

Waterhouse states at the opening that he has decided to climb his grandfather 'free, without a rope or net'. This reflects his use of free verse to write, perhaps mirroring the unplanned nature of memory. As he climbs, he stops en route, again echoing how some memories hold us for longer than others. However, by 'climbing' without safety equipment, Waterhouse may also imply that we may stumble into bad memories, like a crevasse, and fall.

- Opening makes clear reference to the poem
- Links form to theme in task
- Develops idea
- Presents a more complex interpretation

Now you try!

Finish this paragraph about family support. Use one of the quotations from the list.

Waterhouse explores the ways in which older family members support the young, by …

My progress   Needs more work ☐   Getting there ☐   Sorted! ☐

SPECIAL FOCUS 6: Voice and viewpoint

What is voice and viewpoint?

- The **voice** in a poem is the **speaker** or **narrator**.
- The **viewpoint** is the **perspective** that the speaker offers on the theme.

How do I identify them in a poem like 'Climbing My Grandfather'?

- Sometimes, a clear **narrative voice** is identified – here, the title makes clear that the speaker is a grandson.
- If a voice is created using 'I', we can't assume this is the poet's own voice. Even when we know it's (semi-)autobiographical, it's still a created **persona**.
- Viewpoint may be harder to identify. Is Waterhouse adopting the child's viewpoint, or using the **metaphor** to reflect as an adult? Or both?
- Consider **vocabulary** used: here, a child's perspective is created through descriptions of the grandfather's immense size.
- Read the **mood** and **tone**: the shift from active verbs like **'discover'** to more reflective ones like **'feeling'** suggest a change in perspective.

Exam focus

How can I write about viewpoint?

You could use adjectives or adverbs/adjectives to identify viewpoint:
thoughtful, enthusiastic, childish, sombre, cautious.

> The poem begins with an enthusiastic 'scramble' onto the grandfather's lap, suggesting a small child's exploration. However, as the poem develops and the 'climbing' becomes more obviously metaphorical, we see the viewpoint shift to that of an adult understanding the value of his grandfather's 'good heart'.

Anchors viewpoint to key references

Identifies voice/ viewpoint

How viewpoint might change

Now you try!

Think about the other poems in the cluster. Do any use an apparently autobiographical voice or suggest a change of voice?

1. Look at this ideas map representing 'When We Two Parted'. Is there anything else you could add?

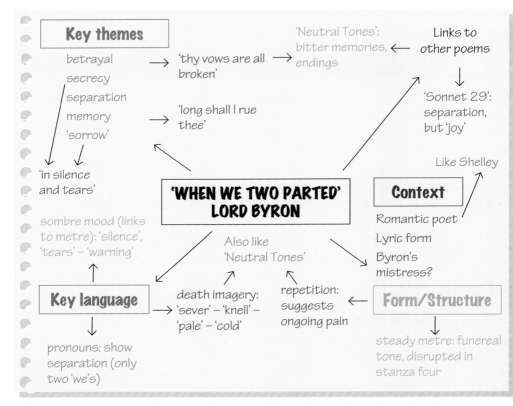

Key themes
- betrayal
- secrecy
- separation
- memory
- 'sorrow'

→ 'thy vows are all broken'

→ 'long shall I rue thee'

'Neutral Tones': bitter memories, ← endings

Links to other poems

↓

'Sonnet 29': separation, but 'joy'

Like Shelley

'in silence and tears'

sombre mood (links to metre): 'silence', 'tears' – 'warning'

'WHEN WE TWO PARTED' LORD BYRON

Context
- Romantic poet
- Lyric form
- Byron's mistress?

Key language

↓

pronouns: show separation (only two 'we's)

Also like 'Neutral Tones'

death imagery: 'sever' – 'knell' – 'pale' – 'cold'

repetition: suggests ongoing pain

Form/Structure

↓

steady metre: funereal tone, disrupted in stanza four

2. Create your own ideas map for one of the other poems from the cluster. Include themes, key language, form/structure, context and links.

Quick quiz

Answer these quick questions about the poems in the anthology:

1. Who is 'feeding words' onto a screen?
2. When do the mother and daughter practise dance steps in 'Before You Were Mine'?
3. What does the father wear for ploughing in 'Follower'?

4. Where do the speaker and his wife sit in the evening in 'Singh Song!'?
5. To what does Byron compare the sound of his lover's name?
6. Name two trees mentioned in 'The Farmer's Bride'.
7. What does Barrett Browning compare her thoughts to in 'Sonnet 29 – "I think of thee!"'?
8. Who compares themselves to a 'parent stem'?
9. What is the name of the poetic form used for 'Porphyria's Lover'?
10. Where does an 'H.P. sauce bottle' feature, and why?
11. What does Waterhouse do when he reaches his grandfather's teeth?
12. Shelley's use of nature imagery is typical of what poetic movement?
13. Why is the sun white in 'Neutral Tones'?
14. Name three things measured in 'Mother, any distance'.
15. Who is the speaker in 'Porphyria's Lover' waiting to hear from, and why?
16. How does the father in 'Follower' measure the earth's furrows?
17. What are the swans compared to in 'Winter Swans'?
18. What hairstyle does the speaker's wife have in 'Singh Song!'?
19. How long has the speaker been married in 'The Farmer's Bride'?
20. Who did Cecil Day Lewis write 'Walking Away' about?

Power paragraphs

Write a paragraph in response to **each of these questions**. Include **one quotation** from each poem.

1. How does Mew use rhyme in 'The Farmer's Bride'?
2. What is the effect of **pathetic fallacy** in 'Porphyria's Lover'?

Exam practice

How does Causley convey love for his parents in 'Eden Rock'?
Write **two paragraphs** explaining your ideas. You could comment on:

- the light imagery and vocabulary he uses
- use of detail.

THEMES Family relationships

Five key things about how the poets explore family relationships

1. **Family relationships** is the central theme in poems such as 'Follower', 'Mother, any distance' and 'Before You Were Mine'.
2. Other poems explore family relationships in **a less direct way**, for instance in 'Eden Rock', where Causley uses **family to explore death and loss**, or 'Singh Song!', which presents **several relationships**.
3. Most of these poems present the **viewpoints of parents or children**, such as the father in 'Walking Away' or the son in 'Mother, any distance'.
4. Other poems explore **extended family relationships**, such as grandson and grandfather in Andrew Waterhouse's 'Climbing My Grandfather'.
5. Family relationships may be presented **positively**, as in 'Before You Were Mine', or **with ambivalence**, as in Heaney's 'Follower'.

How is the child's experience of family conveyed?

- Armitage uses metaphor to explore conflict between the need for parental support and the desire to break free.
- 'Follower' addresses the shift from cared-for to carer that children experience as their parents age.
- Causley uses a memory to explore the abandonment that even adults may feel on the death of parents.
- In 'Singh Song!', Nagra hints at parental pressure through the speaker's experience of family disagreements.

How is the parents' experience of family conveyed?

- In 'Walking Away', Day-Lewis tries to put into words the complex emotions of parents watching their children grow up.
- in 'Before You Were Mine', Duffy imagines how her birth might have affected her mother's experience of life.
- 'Follower' conveys a parent's patience with a child's learning, but through the child's eyes. In 'Mother, any distance', Armitage attempts to portray a mother's yearning to maintain a close mother–child bond.

What different attitudes to family relationships are conveyed?

- 'Climbing My Grandfather' uses mountain and climbing **imagery** to suggest the way that children often look up to and worship grandparents.
- Through an almost photographic image, Causley presents a sense of both love for and distance from his parents in 'Eden Rock'.
- In 'Follower', the speaker shows how early idealisation of a strong father changes as the adult child develops his own identity.

Three key quotations

1. Gratitude: 'You'd teach me the steps on the way home from Mass' ('Before You Were Mine').
2. Anxiety, even guilt: 'I have had worse partings, but none that so / Gnaws at my mind still' ('Walking Away').
3. Frustration: 'I reach towards a hatch that opens on an endless sky' ('Mother, any distance').

Note it!

Notice that the poems focusing on family in the anthology are all more 'modern' poems, and nearly all about parents. Why might that be?

Exam focus

How can I write about relationships? AO1

You can write about a parent's feelings of loss.

Day Lewis makes it clear that he has not been able to forget the memory of parting from his son at school. He says that, while he's had 'worse partings', none of them 'so gnaws at [his] mind still', suggesting the lingering pain the memory causes him. The word 'gnaws' describes a niggling pain, like hunger, implying emptiness or a feeling of incompleteness: perhaps it's also guilt he feels at 'walking away' from his small son when he was so young.	Introduces the core idea
	Apt quotation
	Explains clearly
	Language focus develops and interprets

Now you try!

Write your own paragraph about a different attitude to family in the cluster. Use one of the given quotations.

My progress   Needs more work ☐   Getting there ☐   Sorted! ☐

THEMES Love and desire

Five key things about how the poets explore love and desire

1. Some poems explore **love within marriage**, such as 'The Farmer's Bride' or 'Singh Song!'.
2. Other poems present **love within less 'conventional' relationships**, such as 'Porphyria's Lover', or possibly 'Letters from Yorkshire'.
3. Some poems explore **the effect of physical absence on love**, as Maura Dooley does in 'Letters from Yorkshire' or Barrett Browning in 'Sonnet 29'.
4. **Sexual desire** is explored in 'Porphyria's Lover', 'Singh Song!' and 'Sonnet 29'.
5. Ideas about **the possessive nature of sexual desire** can be found in 'Love's Philosophy', 'Porphyria's Lover' and 'The Farmer's Bride'.

How are positive experiences of love and desire conveyed?

- In 'Singh Song!', the speaker's new bride transports him from the mundanity of his daily life.
- Barrett Browning expresses her passionate love for her husband through natural **imagery** in 'Sonnet 29'.
- Shelley also uses natural imagery in 'Love's Philosophy' to convey the natural goodness of sexual desire, even if his is left unfulfilled.
- Dooley suggests that love is about communication as much as physical presence.

How are negative experiences of love and desire conveyed?

- In 'The Farmer's Bride', Mew explores a young girl's fear of sexual contact and the impact this has on her husband's hopes within marriage.
- In 'Sonnet 29', as well as celebrating love, the speaker expresses frustration at her husband's absence.
- Browning shows the destructive possibilities of sexual desire and obsession through murder in 'Porphyria's Lover'.
- 'Singh Song!' shows how romantic love can struggle against family disapproval through the contrasting attitudes of different generations.

What different attitudes to love and desire are conveyed?

- Using nature imagery, 'Love's Philosophy' presents an argument that being together – and, by implication, sex – is natural and a part of 'divine law'.
- 'The Farmer's Bride' presents the conventions of nineteenth-century marriage through the **voice** of the farmer and his descriptions of his young wife.
- 'Letters from Yorkshire' explores the idea of love as a connection between **'souls'** rather than bodies, never making clear the nature of the relationship.

Three key quotations

1. Fulfilment: 'All things [...] / In one another's being mingle' ('Love's Philosophy').
2. Sexual desire: 'after vee hav made luv / like vee rowing through Putney' ('Singh Song!').
3. Obsession: 'Too weak [...] And give herself to me for ever' ('Porphyria's Lover').

Note it!

What differences and similarities do you see in the ways that pre-twentieth century and contemporary poets explore ideas of marriage and sexual relations?

Exam focus

How can I write about love and desire? AO1 AO2

You can write about attitudes to physical love.

For Shelley, 'Love's Philosophy' is a chance to argue that sexual fulfilment is so natural, the object of his desire shouldn't hesitate to join him. He tries to persuade her that 'all things in one another's being mingle', implying it is natural to become a pair rather than staying single. While 'being' might be understood as a less physical kind of love, the connotations of 'mingle' and earlier references to 'kissing' suggest that it's the fulfilment of his physical desire that he seeks.

- Introduces the core idea
- Apt quotation
- Explains clearly
- Language focus develops and interprets

Now you try!

Write your own paragraph about romantic love or desire in the cluster. Use one of the given quotations.

THEMES Breakdown and betrayal

Five key things about how the poets explore breakdown and betrayal

1. Some poems explore **the breakdown of a relationship in the past**, such as 'When We Two Parted' and 'Neutral Tones'.
2. Other poems present **relationships in current difficulties**, like 'The Farmer's Bride' or 'Wild Swans', with **different prospects for recovery**.
3. Some poems convey ideas about **the falseness of love itself** through **feelings of betrayal**, like 'Porphyria's Lover' or 'Neutral Tones'.
4. Some responses present **bitterness**, like 'When We Two Parted', while others focus on **feelings of sadness**, like 'The Farmer's Bride'.
5. A few poems introduce ideas around **a breakdown in family relationships**, such as 'Singh Song!' or, to some extent, 'Follower'.

How are ideas about the breakdown of love conveyed?

- In 'Neutral Tones', Hardy uses a circular form to represent the hopelessness of dying love.
- Mew uses animal **imagery** in 'The Farmer's Bride' to emphasise the incompatibility in the marriage.
- In 'Winter Swans', the weather hints at the unsettled relationship.
- Byron's insistent **rhythm** in 'When We Two Parted' makes the death of the relationship seem inevitable.

How are feelings inspired by breakdown or betrayal conveyed?

- In 'Porphyria's Lover', Browning's speaker uses repetition to show both anger at Porphyria and satisfaction once her 'betrayal' has been 'resolved'.
- In 'The Farmer's Bride', the speaker's sentences become shorter and more vehement, suggesting barely contained frustration at his situation.
- Hardy's use of death imagery in 'Neutral Tones', from the sun to the tree, echoes the death of feeling in the relationship.
- By ending **stanzas** with questions in 'Love's Philosophy', Shelley implies disbelief that his loved one is 'betraying' natural laws of love by not giving in to him.

What different attitudes to breakdown and betrayal are conveyed?

- 'When We Two Parted' suggests that a lover who breaks **'vows'** can never be trusted again, in the same or a new relationship.
- 'The Farmer's Bride' juxtaposes conventional ideals of being a 'good wife' with the value of personal freedom and the reality of emotional difficulties.
- 'Winter Swans' raises the romantic and religious vow of loving 'until death do us part', like swans who **'mate for life'**. Is the speaker convinced?

Three key quotations

1. Regret: 'When us was wed she turned afraid / Of love and me and all things human' ('The Farmer's Bride').
2. Recrimination: '... words played between us to and fro / On which lost the more by our love' ('Neutral Tones').
3. Bitterness: 'In silence I grieve, / That thy heart could forget' ('When We Two Parted').

Note it!

How do poets present speakers who accept responsibility for the breakdown of a relationship? Do we feel more sympathy for them?

Exam focus

How can I write about the breakdown of a relationship?

You can write about the presentation of blame.

> Thomas Hardy explores ideas of blame at the end of a relationship in 'Neutral Tones', which contrasts with the title's suggestion that he now feels nothing. He describes a meeting in which the couple argue over 'which lost the more by our love', showing the negativity that has overwhelmed the relationship: the word 'lost' shows how this pair have twisted love into its opposite, something 'taking away' rather than 'giving'.

Introduces the core idea

Apt quotation

Explains clearly

Language focus develops and interprets

Now you try!

Write your own paragraph about a bitter response to relationship breakdown in the cluster. Use one of the given quotations.

THEMES Time and memory

Five key things about how the poets explore time and memory

1. The poets explore **the effect of time on both romantic love** – as in 'Neutral Tones' – **and family relationships** – as in 'Follower'.

2. Some poems use **the idea of memory** to consider **how relationships change**, such as 'Walking Away' or 'Eden Rock'.

3. Other poems explore children's **changing emotions** about **parents as they grow up**, like 'Mother, any Distance' and 'Before You Were Mine'.

4. Some poems present **emotions caused by time spent apart**, such as **impatience** in 'Sonnet 29' or **reflection** in 'Letters from Yorkshire'.

5. Some poems focus on **the memory of a particular person**: a **past lover** in 'Neutral Tones', a **grandparent** in 'Climbing my Grandfather'.

How is the impact of time on relationships conveyed?

- In 'Mother, any distance', Armitage uses an **extended metaphor** of a cord to represent both close ties and the growing distance between mother and son.

- Browning uses a shift in **narrative** focus from 'she' to 'I' in 'Porphyria's Lover' to explore how a relationship can change in a heartbeat.

- In 'Eden Rock', Causley's final, single-line **stanza** emphasises the distance between parents and adult child.

- Mew's use of seasonal **imagery** in 'The Farmer's Bride' reflects the passing of time and growing coldness in the marriage.

How are memories of love conveyed?

- In 'Climbing My Grandfather', Waterhouse's use of physical details suggests how lovingly he remembers every inch of his grandfather.

- Byron's repetition of **'silence and tears'** in 'When We Two Parted' shows that memories of a past relationship have not softened over time.

- Causley's use of light imagery in 'Eden Rock' recalls a hazy old photograph, perhaps reminding us that all we can keep of love are memories.

- In 'Neutral Tones', Hardy's stilted **rhythms** hint at the discomfort he feels in recalling the end of the relationship.

What different attitudes to the effects of time on love are conveyed?

- 'Before You Were Mine' plays with the idea that children destroy their parents' dreams unwittingly by taking away **'fizzy, movie tomorrows'**.
- 'The Farmer's Bride' explores ideas of patience as the farmer waits longingly for his frightened wife to spend more time in his company.
- 'Neutral Tones' suggests that time can 'shape' our memories of love, twisting them to reflect present feelings.

Three key quotations

1. Change: 'I'm not here yet. The thought of me doesn't occur' ('Before You Were Mine').
2. Reopening wounds: 'It felt like the warning / Of what I feel now' ('When We Two Parted').
3. Feelings of loss in a memory: 'like a satellite / Wrenched from its orbit' ('Walking Away').

Note it!

How far do you feel the poems validate the idea that 'time heals'? Is this equally true of older and more modern poems?

Exam focus

How can I write about reflecting on love after time has passed? **AO1**

You can write about the recurring pain of loss.

Byron suggests that the pain he is now feeling is a return to the pain he first felt when the relationship ended: 'It felt like the warning / Of what I feel now'. 'Feel' echoes 'felt', emphasising how his present feelings are the same as the past ones. In fact, he implies, the pain of hearing about her now is worse, since the pain of parting was only a 'warning', implying now the pain is for real.

| Paraphrases core idea |
| Quotation supports |
| Explains clearly |
| Language focus develops and interprets |

Now you try!

Write your own paragraph about the a memory of a loss in the cluster. Use one of the given quotations.

THEMES Nature

Five key things about how the poets explore nature

1. Some poems *state* the idea that love is natural, like 'Love's Philosophy' or 'Winter Swans'.
2. Other poems *imply* that love is natural, such as 'Sonnet 29' or perhaps 'Climbing My Grandfather'.
3. Some poems use **nature imagery** to explore **themes around love and relationships**, such as 'Walking Away' or 'Neutral Tones'.
4. Other poems use **nature as a physical setting**, such as 'Wild Swans' or 'Porphyria's Lover'.
5. In 'The Farmer's Bride' and 'Letters from Yorkshire', the **speaker or other character is linked to nature** themselves and **appear to embody it**.

How do poets use nature to explore love?

- In 'Sonnet 29,' Barrett Browning uses the imagery of the palm-tree and vine to illustrate her overwhelming passion for her husband.
- In 'Neutral Tones', Hardy's use of dead and ominous nature imagery echoes the speaker's negative emotions about the relationship.
- Heaney's childhood devotion to his father is represented by the detailed farming and sea imagery he uses to describe him in 'Follower'.
- In 'Porphyria's Lover', the disruptive storm outside could reflect the wild and destructive character of Browning's speaker through **pathetic fallacy**.

How are links between relationships and nature explored?

- A vision of swans is presented by Sheers as helping a struggling couple bridge the distance between them.
- Mew's speaker in 'The Farmer's Bride' compares his wife to wild animals and respects her **'wild self'**, suggesting he does not wish to harm her.
- Waterhouse's use of landscape imagery in 'Climbing My Grandfather' hints at the enduring nature of his love for both his grandfather and the countryside.
- In 'Letters from Yorkshire', the addressee's closeness to nature makes Dooley worry that his life is more **'real'**, voicing her insecurities within the relationship.

74

What different attitudes to love being natural are conveyed?

- 'Love's Philosophy' argues that human sexuality and love are 'natural' by comparing human relationships to connections in the natural world, e.g. the way the sun 'kisses' the earth.
- In 'The Farmer's Bride', Mew may question the idea that a **'wild'** and free nature must be tamed by marriage and domesticity.
- The nature setting in 'Eden Rock' could suggest that death is 'natural', as is the sadness that accompanies loss of loved ones.

Quick quiz

Answer these quick questions about the poems in the anthology:

1. Which poem uses mountain imagery?
2. Name two poems that offer a child's perspective.
3. Which poems explore love in marriage?
4. In which poem is a parent compared to a film star?
5. Which poems suggest that love is natural?
6. Name two poems that describe someone who works on the land.
7. In which poem does the speaker try to persuade someone to kiss them?
8. Which poem presents obsessive love?
9. In 'Winter Swans', what do the swans symbolise?
10. Name four different relationships that appear in the cluster.

Exam practice

Write a paragraph about one poet's attitude to nature in the cluster. Make sure you **use one quotation**.

EXAM PRACTICE Understanding the exam

Five key things about Paper 1 Section B

1. You will have **one** question on 'Love and Relationships' which will be based on **a poem from the Anthology** which will be **printed** on the **exam paper**, and **another of your choosing** (also from the **Anthology**).

2. You will be asked to **compare** how the **poets** of the given poem and the one you choose **present** ideas on a particular **theme** or **issue**.

3. You will have about **40 minutes** to read and respond to the question.

4. The question is worth **30 marks**.

5. The question assesses **AOs 1, 2 and 3**. Remember that **AO3** relates to 'context'.

What will a question look like?

You must look at similarities and differences

Compare the ways the poets present ideas about separation in 'The Farmer's Bride' and in one other poem from 'Love & Relationships'.

You must explain the techniques the two poets use

The other poem is one you should choose from the Anthology

This named poem is the one you are given in the exam paper

This is the theme, idea or issue you should look for

Do all questions look the same?

- The question might be worded slightly differently, for example: **Compare how poets present strong feelings in 'Sonnet 29' and in one other poem from 'Love and Relationships'**.

- Whatever the precise wording, you will need to **compare** how **two poets present** a **theme or idea**, and the **ways** in which they do it, i.e. the **methods/techniques** they use.

What do I need to do to get a good mark?

Use this grid to understand your current level and how to improve it:

	AO1 Read, understand, respond	**AO2** Analyse language, form, structure and effects	**AO3** Show understanding of contexts
High	• You make **precise comparisons** between the **two poems**. Your argument is **well-structured**, with quotations **fluently embedded** in sentences.	• You **analyse** and **interpret** the **methods** the **two poets** use **very effectively**. You explore **thoughtfully** the effects of these on the reader. You show **excellent use of poetic terminology**.	• You make **detailed relevant links** between specific elements of the poems and **social, historical contexts** relevant to the **core issue**.
Mid	• You make a **range of references** when comparing the two poems. • You respond in a **clear, logical way** with **relevant quotations** chosen.	• You **explain clearly** some of the methods the poets use, and **some effects** on the reader. • You use **mostly relevant poetic terminology**.	• You show **clear evidence** of understanding **context** which is **linked** to the poems in **places**.
Lower	• You make **some references** to the poems, but in rather a **patchy** way, with **little direct comparison**. • You make **some useful points** but evidence is **not always clear** or **relevant**.	• You make **occasional attempts** to explain the poets' methods but these are a **little unclear**. • You show **some** use of **poetic terminology**.	• You demonstrate **basic awareness of context** but **links** to the poems are **undeveloped** and **not always relevant**.

EXAM PRACTICE Planning and writing your response

Re-read the question below and the poem it mentions (see pages 28–31).

Compare the ways the poets present ideas about separation in 'The Farmer's Bride' and in one other poem from 'Love and Relationships'.

[30 marks]

Five key stages to follow

1. **Read** the **question**; **highlight** key words.
2. **Choose** the **poem** you will compare/contrast the given poem with.
3. **Annotate** the poem printed **on the exam paper**; and **make notes** on the **second poem**.
4. **Plan** for paragraphs.
5. **Write** your response; **check it** against your plan/notes as you progress.

What should I focus on?

Highlight the **key words**:

Compare the ways the poets present ideas about separation in 'The Farmer's Bride' and in one other poem from 'Love and Relationships'.

What do they tell you? You must comment on **both** poems, looking for **similarities** and **differences** with regard to the theme of 'separation'. Explain what **methods** each poet uses.

How should I use the given poem?

- Check for any clear links to the question (e.g. the wife avoids her husband).
- Highlight any words, phrases or methods you could use (e.g. **'Not near, not near!'** – wife actively avoids men).

How do I make notes on the poem I have chosen?

- Find any links between the poem you have chosen and the notes you have made on the given poem.
- Write these as a separate list next to the given poem.

What poetic techniques should I look for?

Look for a range of techniques in both poems. These could include:

- powerful **single words** or **phrases** (**'Oh! my God!'**)
- distinctive use of **voice** (the farmer's use of nature **imagery** which fits his role)
- aspects of **form** or **structure**; use of **verses**, **repetition**, **line length**, **tenses**, etc. (e.g. how the repeated final phrase **'her hair'** suggests his longing for closeness)
- **poetic devices** such as **assonance**, **enjambment**, **alliteration**, imagery, etc. (symbolism of hunting, long vowels of rhymes).

How do I structure my response?

- Plan to **write 4–5 points** on **each poem**.
- **Choose a structure** that suits you. You could:

  Option 1: Write about the **first poem in full** then **the second** (but can be more difficult to compare).

  Option 2: Write **alternate paragraphs** with different points on each poem (e.g. Poem A, Poem B, Poem A, Poem B).

  Option 3: Write **paragraphs where you refer between the poems** constantly (e.g. Poem A and B, Poem A and B, etc.).

How do I compare effectively?

If you choose method 3 you will need to compare within paragraphs, choosing appropriate connective words or phrases. For example:

Throughout the poem, the farmer compares his wife to a wild animal, 'shy as a leveret', implying he feels guilt at 'chasing' her and emphasising his feelings of separation from her. By contrast, in 'Winter Swans', the speaker's symbol of the swans who 'mate for life' implies that they are both like swans, suggesting that they are similar and will not be separated for long.

Explains where in poem

Evidence and effect

Connectives draw comparison with second poem

Now you try!

Take the same question (on 'The Farmer's Bride') and choose your own poem to compare. Make notes and plan a response, deciding how you will structure your essay (see the three methods suggested).

What does a Grade 5 answer look like?

Read the task and the poem again, then the sample answer below.

> Compare the ways the poets present ideas about separation in 'The Farmer's Bride' and in one other poem from 'Love and Relationships'.
>
> **[30 marks]**

In 'The Farmer's Bride', the speaker is a farmer who has married, but finds his wife doesn't want to be around him. She's so scared of him, he even describes how she 'runned away'. The speaker doesn't say exactly, but we can guess she doesn't like the physical side of marriage because she doesn't want men near her and has slept alone 'in the attic'. In 'Winter Swans', however, the couple are together, but they've had an argument. Sheers says they are walking 'silent and apart'. This suggests they feel separate from each other at this moment, rather than three years of feeling separate, like the farmer.

AO1 clear statement links to theme of separation

AO2 references from text add detail

AO1 comparison with second poem

The farmer in 'The Farmer's Bride' seems to be very patient with his wife, but he chased her when she ran away. 'And turned the key upon her, fast' sounds like he's trapped her. He compares her to wild animals like 'a leveret', like he wants to tame her to stop the separation between them. This shows he has more power. The relationship in 'Winter Swans' seems more equal, however. Perhaps this is because it's written at a time when men and women are more equal in relationships, whereas in Mew's day, marriage was for life.

AO2 more detailed use of language with effects explained

AO3 relevant context raised, though not entirely clear

Charlotte Mew uses lots of nature imagery in 'The Farmer's Bride' to show the speaker's background as a farmer. He talks about the seasons changing, saying 'the short days shorten'. This indicates that time is always moving on, but he thinks that his marriage isn't.

AO2 mentions effect of language but no comparison to second poem for AO1

Both poems include ideas about silence to show separation. In 'The Farmer's Bride', his wife communicates with her eyes only. He says she is 'like a mouse' when she does housework, suggesting she's so quiet you don't notice her. In 'Winter Swans', it's a different kind of silence, maybe an angry one after an argument, rather than because the woman is scared of the man, who had more power in marriage then. But the main difference is that at the end, the speaker's girlfriend breaks the silence by commenting on the swans and how 'they mate for life', unlike the farmer's wife, who won't speak to him.

Paragraph 4

The fact both poems end differently is also important. At the end of 'Winter Swans', because of what she says, the couple reach out to each other – their hands have 'swum the distance' between them. This implies that they have come together again, equally. In 'The Farmer's Bride', however, the farmer gets more upset as you can tell from his exclamations like 'Oh! my God!' He thinks about his wife, still separate up the stairs. It ends with him dreaming of her softness and beauty. He can't stop thinking about it, which suggests he won't be able to stay separate long, but it still won't be what his wife wants.

Paragraph 5

Check the skills

Re-read paragraphs four and five of this response and:
- highlight **comparative points** made about the poems
- circle any reference to **context**
- underline any places where the student has made an **interpretation**.

Now you try!

Look again at paragraph three and improve it by:
- **adding a quotation** from the **second poem** to support the comparison point
- **explaining more clearly** how nature imagery could link to ideas of separation
- **improving** the **overall style** by using **connectives** to link or **compare/contrast points**.

Re-read the task and the poem, then the sample answer below.

> Compare the ways the poets present ideas about separation in 'The Farmer's Bride' and in one other poem from 'Love and Relationships'.
>
> **[30 marks]**

Reading 'The Farmer's Bride' and 'Letters from Yorkshire' side by side emphasises the many ways we can experience separation, physically or emotionally, within a relationship and, despite the different times of writing, the poets share an understanding of the complex thoughts involved.

AO1 clear linking of both poems to theme (AO3)

On the surface, the poems show reverse situations. Mew's farmer has lived with his young wife 'three summers since', yet she chooses to keep away from him, sleeping 'up in the attic there alone'. Dooley describes a pair – although the nature of the relationship is never made explicit – who, although separated by 'icy miles', maintain communication through letters which bring 'air and light' to the speaker, nourishing the relationship and keeping it alive. The farmer, on the other hand, feels the disappearance of his wife's smile 'like the shut of a winter day', suggesting his feelings of cold and darkness. She may be literally locked in the house, but it's he who feels entombed in a dead marriage.

AO1 development of argument

AO2 detailed examination of language

AO2 insightful interpretation

Winter appears as a setting in both poems, in fact, with Dooley's addressee 'digging' in the garden, 'knuckles singing as they reddened in the warmth'; here, winter brings a kind of exhilaration to life, reminding us of the new life he is 'planting' in the garden. For the speaker in 'The Farmer's Bride', also, the bareness of winter may echo the desolate separation of his marriage, but as 'the berries redden' before Christmas, he can't help thinking of new life, either. Both poems, then, suggest possibilities of joy or reconciliation.

AO1 comparison developed

AO1 **AO3** mid-essay comparison linked back to theme for clear argument and contextual point

Overall, though, the tone created by each poet suggests very different outcomes. Dooley describes the constant communication between the separated pair, suggesting it's a practical necessity and 'simply how things are', which they manage. It doesn't stop their 'souls tap[ping] out messages' to each other; they feel together. In 'The Farmer's Bride', however, there's a darker edge to the speaker's patient understanding as he grapples with loneliness. He knows his wife is a gentle, 'wild' creature. But in the final stanza, where constricted phrases and repetition suggest urgency and obsessive thoughts of her 'soft ... brown' body, Mew indicates his desire to hunt and master.

Paragraph 4

Mew's sensitive presentation of feelings of separation is a reminder that she herself often felt alienated from social norms, either through the mental health issues that troubled her or through her unconventional living choices. Her speaker feels separated both from his wife and a society that expects him to dominate, helping him 'chase' and hunt down the girl when she first escapes. It's a far cry from the relationship of equals, separated by individual choices, depicted by Dooley.

Paragraph 5

Check the skills

Re-read paragraphs four and five of this response and:

- identify any particularly **fluent** or **well-expressed comparisons or contrasts** between the poems
- find any further references to **context**
- highlight any places where the student has shown **deeper insight** and offered **original** or particularly **thoughtful** ideas or made interesting **links**.

Now you try!

Now, plan and write **two paragraphs** in response to this new task, using the skills you have learned.

> Compare how the poets present memories of love in 'Neutral Tones' and one other poem from 'Love and Relationships'.

- Try to match your paragraphs to the High Level objectives on page 77.

Now you try!

- Decode the question by highlighting the key words.
- Annotate the given poem with points related to the question.
- Choose your second poem and add annotations related to it.
- Plan your points and select your quotations.
- Write your answer.
- Look at the suggested list of key points in the **Answers** (page 88).

Compare how the poets present attitudes to a family member in 'Climbing My Grandfather' and **one** other poem in 'Love and Relationships'.

[30 marks]

I decide to do it free, without a rope or net.
First, the old brogues, dusty and cracked;
an easy scramble onto his trousers,
pushing into the weave, trying to get a grip.
5   By the overhanging shirt I change
direction, traverse along his belt
to an earth-stained hand. The nails
are splintered and give good purchase,
the skin of his finger is smooth and thick
10 like warm ice. On his arm I discover
the glassy ridge of a scar, place my feet
gently in the old stitches and move on.
At his still firm shoulder, I rest for a while
in the shade, not looking down,
15 for climbing has its dangers, then pull
myself up the loose skin of his neck
to a smiling mouth to drink among teeth.
Refreshed, I cross the screed cheek,
to stare into his brown eyes, watch a pupil
20 slowly open and close. Then up over
the forehead, the wrinkles well-spaced
and easy, to his thick hair (soft and white
at this altitude), reaching for the summit,
where gasping for breath I can only lie
25 watching clouds and birds circle,
feeling his heat, knowing
the slow pulse of his good heart.

GLOSSARY

Literary or language terms	Explanation
alliteration	where the same sound is repeated in a stretch of language, usually at the beginning of words
anapaest (anapaestic metre)	metrical foot of two short or unstressed syllables followed by one long or stressed syllable (xx/)
assonance	when the same vowel sound appears in the same place in a series of words
connotation	an additional meaning attached to a word in specific circumstances, i.e. what it suggests or implies
dactyl (dactylic metre)	metrical foot of stressed long syllable followed by two unstressed syllables (/xx)
dialect	accent and vocabulary, varying by region and social background
dramatic monologue	poetic form written as a character, in which the speaker reveals their 'true' character
end-stopping	when punctuation coincides with the end of the poetic line
enjambment	in poetry when a line runs on into the next line without pause, carrying the thought with it; sometimes called a run-on line
extended metaphor	in poetry, a metaphor that continues some aspect of the image; it may continue into the next line or throughout the poem
figurative	like 'metaphorical', contrasted with 'literal'
foreshadowing	a hint of what is to come in a work of poetry, fiction or drama
free verse	a form of poetry; verses without regular rhythm or pattern, though they may contain some patterns, such as rhyme or repetition
iamb (iambic metre)	metrical foot consisting of a weak syllable followed by a strong one (x/)
iambic pentameter or tetrameter	a line of poetry consisting of five or four iambs
imagery	descriptive language that uses images to make actions, objects and characters more vivid in the reader's mind
juxtaposition	putting two things side by side in order to invite comparison
lyric	a poem, simple or complex, expressing the emotions and thoughts of the speaker often exploring a single feeling or idea
metaphor	when one thing is used to describe another to create a striking or unusual image
metre	the pattern of beats or 'feet' in a line of verse; see also rhythm, anapaest, dactyl, trochee, iamb
metrical foot	unit of rhythm consisting of two or three syllables (one of them stressed), making up the metre
mood	the tone or atmosphere created by an artistic work
motif	recurring theme or pattern in a work of art
narrative	a story

Literary or language terms	Explanation
octave	a verse of eight lines, usually in iambic pentameter; the first eight lines of a sonnet (where it is sometimes called two quatrains)
paradox	absurd or contradictory statement that may still make sense
pathetic fallacy	like 'personification' – used for inanimate objects
pentameter	a line of poetry consisting of five stressed beats
personification	the treatment or description of an object or idea as though they were human, with human feelings and attributes
plosive	consonant sound; in English, p, t, k, b, d and g are all plosives
quatrain	four lines of verse: can stand alone or be repeated
refrain	repeated lines or groups of words that convey the same meaning
rhetorical (question)	asked for effect rather than for an answer
rhyming couplet	a couplet (two paired lines) that rhymes
rhythm	pattern of stressed and unstressed beats in a line of poetry; see also metre
Romantic (movement)	an artistic movement that flourished in the late eighteenth to the mid nineteenth century and valued the personal, individual, the imagination and intense feeling
run-on (line)	when an unpunctuated line 'runs' into the next. See enjambment
semantic field	a set of words grouped by meaning, e.g. light-related
sestet	a verse of six lines; second section (lines 9–14) of traditional sonnet.
sibilance	a type of consonance, with the 's' sound
simile	when one thing is compared directly with another using 'like' or 'as'
sonnet	a fourteen-line verse with a rhyming couplet at the end
stanza	a group or pattern of lines forming a verse
symbol	something that represents something else, usually with meanings that are widely known (e.g. a dove as a symbol of peace)
tercet	a verse of three lines
tetrameter	a line of poetry consisting of four stressed beats
tone	See mood
trochee (trochaic metre)	metrical foot consisting of one stressed syllable followed by one unstressed (/x)
voice	the speaker or narrator of a poem or work of fiction. This persona is created in the speaker's mind, though sometimes it can seem close to the poet's or writer's own voice
volta	the turn or shift in a sonnet (usually after the octave), when a second idea or mood is introduced

ANSWERS

Note that the sample paragraphs given here provide only one possible approach to each task. Many other approaches would also be valid and appropriate.

POEMS

'When We Two Parted' – Now you try! (page 7)

Byron implies that the speaker's lover has betrayed him. He does this by talking about 'vows', which has connotations of oath-taking, with bad luck befalling anyone who goes back on their word. By describing her 'vows' as 'all broken', he suggests they are beyond mending, perhaps also implying that he remains true to his word, unlike her: he is almost accusing her of betraying the very idea of love.

'Love's Philosophy' – Now you try! (page 10)

Shelley suggests that, without love, life is meaningless. He lists all the 'mixing' that goes on in life, building up his argument, before ending with a question: 'What are all these kissings worth if thou kiss not me?' He implies that there is no point in this wonderful life he has just described unless she returns his love. By ending with a question, he also suggests the only 'right' answer is a kiss.

'Porphyria's Lover' – Now you try! (page 15)

Browning's language reveals that the speaker wishes to have power over Porphyria. He says that she is not 'free' to love him, implying she is trapped by other circumstances. However, he seems just as keen to trap her when he imagines that she longs to 'give herself to me for ever'. Browning shows how the speaker's jealousy means he can only see her as a possession, one he wishes to keep.

'Sonnet 29' – Now you try! (page 18)

Barrett Browning shows how much she values the idea of marriage. She describes 'this deep joy' that she feels for her husband, with 'joy' implying almost religious love. This ties in with the religious imagery that she uses elsewhere in the poem of the palm-tree and vine. The fact that her husband brings her 'deep joy' hints at the satisfaction and completion she finds in marriage, where she is happy to live 'within [his] shadow'.

'Neutral Tones' – Now you try! (page 22)

Hardy uses negative vocabulary associated with death. He describes her smile as 'the deadest thing', which is an odd phrase, because it's as if he is saying she is the most dead thing in that dead scene. Moreover, the juxtaposition of 'smile' and 'deadest' turns something joyful into something hideous, like a grinning skull, and the fact he now remembers her smile as 'dead' reveals how his memories have become twisted.

'Letters from Yorkshire' – Now you try! (page 26)

Dooley suggests that having different backgrounds doesn't always matter in a relationship. She states that their 'souls' are connected, even though they appear to lead separate lives. Although she asks herself if his life is 'more real because you dig and sow', while she writes on a screen, she knows that he doesn't believe that. This suggests that they both feel it's their relationship that is 'real', not the differences between them.

'The Farmer's Bride' – Now you try! (page 31)

Mew shows the speaker's desire, as he describes 'the soft young down' of his young wife. Throughout the poem, he compares her to a wild animal, highlighting her difference. Here, desperate for love, he imagines being able to stroke her, like a wild animal. But the fact he still describes her 'down' rather than 'skin' suggests he knows she will never accept him or love him the way he wants.

'Walking Away' – Now you try! (page 35)

Day Lewis explores a child's need for independence in a relationship through his description of the need to develop 'selfhood'. The word 'selfhood' implies that a child is not yet fully formed and can only truly develop and become a 'person' themselves if their parents accept them 'walking away'. A child needs to be able to talk about 'myself' and make their own choices in order to become an adult one day.

'Eden Rock' – Now you try! (page 39)

Causley presents parental love, by imagining his parents waiting across a stream for him. He describes hearing them call from the other side: they tell him that 'Crossing is not as hard as you might think'. The reassurance they offer shows that he imagines his parents still caring for his safety and protecting him from danger or fear, as if he were still a small child, even though they are dead and he is grown-up.

'Follower' – Now you try! (page 43)

Heaney shows how parents support their children, by describing how his father 'rode me on his back'. Most children remember being given piggy-backs when they were small, enjoying the closeness to their parents, but Heaney's father does it even while he is hard at work. The metaphor suggests how, even when struggling themselves, parents 'carry' their children, which makes his ageing father's weakness at the end of the poem all the more poignant.

'Mother, any distance' – Now you try! (page 46)

The poet suggests that it is important for parents to let their children explore. This is presented through Armitage's imagery, for instance in the way he describes 'the acres' and 'prairies' of the new house. The language links to ideas of the 'pioneers' in America who went to find freedom by 'going West'. This suggests that adult children need freedom to explore new territory by moving out of home.

'Before You Were Mine' – Now you try! (page 51)

Carol Ann Duffy explores ideas of possessive love through constant references to her mother as 'mine', suggesting ownership. Linked to this, she describes a baby's first wail as a 'loud, possessive yell', as if, the moment a child is born, it ties its parents to itself with the emotional pull of its crying. Duffy's phrasing suggests that, in this, even though they're physically helpless, babies have power over their parents.

'Winter Swans' – Now you try! (page 55)

Sheers explores ideas about communication in a relationship by using a lakeside setting. He describes how the couple 'skirted' it, as if they are treading carefully around it because they don't want to disturb the temporary stillness. However, the stillness could mask unspoken feelings waiting below their silence, suggesting that, unless the couple communicate, these hidden problems won't go away: they will just surface later.

'Singh Song!' – Now you try! (page 59)

Nagra's speaker presents the romantic idea that love is worth more than anything by using words relating to value at the end of the poem. The couple joke about the 'cost' of the moon, knowing that, like love, it is 'priceless'. Even though each of them spends the day thinking about money, either in the shop or online, this suggests they both know that it is love that makes them happy.

'Climbing My Grandfather' – Now you try! (page 62)

Waterhouse explores the ways in which older family members support the young, by comparing his grandfather to a mountain. By using his grandfather to climb upwards, the speaker implies how his grandfather offers himself wholly to help his grandson without complaint. Along the way, different body parts become metaphors for this support, 'his still firm shoulder' providing physical and mental rest to the speaker before he continues his metaphorical journey.

Quick revision – Quick quiz (pages 64–65)

1. Speaker in 'Letters from Yorkshire'. 2. Mass. 3. Hob-nailed shoes. 4. On his silver stool, behind the chocolate bars. 5. A knell. 6. Larch; oaks. 7. Vines. 8. The speaker in 'Walking Away'. 9. Dramatic monologue. 10. 'Eden Rock', to hold the milk. 11. Stops to drink. 12. Romantic. 13. It's been chidden/cursed by God. 14. Any three from: windows; pelmets; doors; walls; floors. 15. God, because he's murdered someone. 16. With one eye. 17. Icebergs; boats; porcelain. 18. Red crew-cut. 19. Almost three years. 20. His son, Sean.

Quick revision – Power paragraphs (page 65)

1. Mew uses rhyme throughout 'The Farmer's Bride'. At the end of each stanza, rhyming couplets signal the 'end' of a section of the narrative, for instance when the men chase and bring home the wife 'at last' and keep her 'fast': it's as if the farmer is pausing to reflect on the past. However, in the last stanza, there is no final couplet, perhaps echoing the farmer's lack of 'completion' in marriage, and hinting at the wife's uncertain future.

2. At the start of 'Porphyria's Lover', Browning creates a restless tone through his use of pathetic fallacy: the wind is 'sullen', full of 'spite' and a desire to 'vex', suggesting destructive anger. Perhaps the speaker feels he is a victim of Porphyria's 'spite' in deserting him. However, when she 'shut the cold out' on arrival, Browning seems to indicate that, in fact, it's the speaker who is full of anger, creating an ominous mood.

Quick revision – Exam practice (page 65)

You could discuss:

- Causley's light imagery – describing how his mother's hair 'takes on the light' is reminiscent of a halo, suggesting he looks up to her
- the precise description – highlighting details of his father's 'Irish Tweed' suit or the 'tin cups painted blue' could imply the care the speaker takes to keep his memory of his parents alive.

THEMES

Family relationships – Now you try! (page 67)

Simon Armitage explores the frustration an adult child may feel at a parent's over-protective love. Using the metaphor of a house to represent the shared experience of mother and son, he describes reaching the roof 'hatch' and seeing 'an endless sky' beyond. The image of a square of blue sky suggests longing for freedom from the mother's care, and mingled excitement and fear at the 'endless' possibilities if he does so.

Love and desire – Now you try! (page 69)

In 'Singh Song!', Nagra presents the speaker's gleeful desire for his 'newly' wife. He sneaks off from his shopkeeping duties to see her. He compares making 'luv', a romantic euphemism for sex, to 'rowing', which makes it sound both comical and energetic, and suggests they both take pleasure in it. 'Putney' is a staging post in a traditional English boat race, but it's also Hindi for 'wife': perhaps Nagra is sending up national stereotypes about attitudes to sex.

Breakdown and betrayal – Now you try! (page 71)

Byron focuses on the speaker's enforced 'silence' in 'When We Two Parted', unable to talk of his past love for an unknown reason. This seems to make him more bitter that 'thy heart could forget', he complains, contrasting his own grief with her lack of care. The phrasing reminds us that he could not forget, implying bitterness at their different attitudes to past love and a sense of betrayal at her lack of care.

Time and memory – Now you try! (page 73)

Day Lewis uses a metaphor to show the pain of seeing his son 'walk away', using the term 'wrenched' to convey the idea of violent dislocation, even amputation. Although he's recalling a memory, the pain he felt is still vivid, suggesting how time has not lessened it. By comparing his son to a 'satellite', he suggests he was the planet around which his son 'orbited', showing how time has changed earlier patterns in the relationship.

Quick revision – Quick quiz – Themes (page 75)

1.'Climbing My Grandfather'. 2. Any two from: 'Mother, any distance'; 'Before You Were Mine'; 'Follower'; 'Eden Rock'; 'Singh Song!'. 3.'Sonnet 29'; 'The Farmer's Bride'; 'Singh Song!'. 4. Marilyn Monroe in 'Before You Were Mine'. 5. 'Love's Philosophy'; 'Sonnet 29'; 'Winter Swans'. 6. Any two from: 'Letters from Yorkshire'; 'The Farmer's Bride'; 'Follower'. 7. 'Love's Philosophy'. 8. 'Porphyria's Lover'. 9. Lifelong/enduring love. 10. Any four from: lovers; husband and wife; mother/father and daughter/son; grandfather and grandson.

Quick revision – Exam practice (page 75)

Hardy's dismal descriptions of nature in 'Neutral Tones' reflect a bleak view of life overall. In the speaker's memory, the leaves are 'grey' and the sun 'white', and the only bird is 'ominous': he sees nothing beautiful in the winter scene, because his emotions have drained it of colour. This suggests that, in the absence of human affection, nature holds no comfort, and life itself is deadened.

EXAM PRACTICE

Planning and writing your response – Now you try! (page 79)

Answers will vary for this task.

Grade 5 answer – Check the skills (page 81)

- **Comparative points:** Both poems include ideas about silence to show separation; the fact both poems end differently is also important.
- **Context:** In 'Winter Swans', it's a different kind of silence, maybe an angry one after an argument, rather than because the woman is scared of the man, who had more power in marriage then.
- **Interpretation:** He says she is 'like a mouse' when she does housework, suggesting she's so quiet, you don't notice her; their hands have 'swum the distance' between them. This implies that they have come together again, equally; He can't stop thinking about it, which suggests he won't be able to stay separate long.

Grade 5 answer – Now you try! (page 81)

Charlotte Mew uses lots of nature imagery in 'The Farmer's Bride' to show the speaker's background as a farmer. When he talks about the seasons changing, saying 'the short days shorten', it shows that time is always moving on, but he thinks that his marriage isn't. He feels separate from his wife, comparing her to wild animals, which shows how different he feels they are, as she prefers to be with the cows. However, in 'Winter

Swans', the male speaker sees how 'the swans came and stopped us'. It's as though he sees the swans as a reflection of both of them, implying they are close, whereas the farmer sees his wife as almost a different species to him.

Grade 7+ answer – Check the skills (page 83)

- **Comparisons:** the tone created by each poet suggests very different outcomes; It doesn't stop their 'souls tap[ping] out messages' to each other; they feel together. In 'The Farmer's Bride', however, there's a darker edge to the speaker's patient understanding as he grapples with loneliness; It's a far cry from the relationship of equals, separated by individual choices, depicted by Dooley.
- **Context:** she herself often felt alienated from social norms, either through the mental health issues that troubled her or through her unconventional living choices. Her speaker feels separated both from his wife and a society that expects him to dominate.
- **Deeper insight:** He knows his wife is a gentle, 'wild' creature. But in the final stanza, where constricted phrases and repetition suggest urgency and obsessive thoughts of her 'soft … brown' body, Mew indicates his desire to hunt and master.

Grade 7+ answer – Now you try! (page 83)

Example answer:

- Hardy's 'death' imagery creates a mood of bitterness and lifelessness, e.g. 'the starving sod'.
- This contrasts with Day Lewis's tender tone in 'Walking Away', with imagery of new life.
- Hardy's use of circular form suggests he is unable to move on. Hardy views his memories as blighted by love: 'keen lessons that love deceives […] have shaped to me Your face'.
- Day Lewis's poem focuses on themes of 'letting go', with a sense of what he has learned.

Practice question (page 84)

Example:

- AO1: Waterhouse presents his grandfather as a calm, working man with 'earth-stained hand', whereas Duffy sees her mother as 'glamorous' in 'Before You Were Mine'.
- AO1: there's a mood of nostalgia in Duffy, also, for lost opportunities to get to know younger versions of loved family members.
- AO2: Waterhouse uses landscape and natural imagery – 'screed cheek' – to characterise his grandfather while Duffy references Hollywood imagery – 'Marilyn', 'pavement' stars – to depict her mother.
- AO2: both poets show powerful admiration for their grandfather/mother through their language, which suggests modest backgrounds but strong character.
- AO3: there is something almost romantic in the way that Duffy presents her mother, a reminder of the complex nature of love.